IT'S NOT A SECRET UNLESS YOU SHARE IT . . .

More hilarious secrets from
I Forgot to Wear Underwear on a Glass-Bottom Boat

- The woman who spent an entire day working at the wrong company

- A bride-to-be who secretly plans on being a virgin forever

- The veteran accountant who adds and subtracts on her fingers and toes

- The cat owner who gets sky-high on catnip

- The man who trained his neighbor's dog to annoy his master

- The woman who broke wind and scared away a burglar

- The man who can't get rid of his erection

I forgot to wear underwear on a glass-bottom boat:

REAL PEOPLE, TRUE SECRETS

Peter & Susan Fenton

St. Martin's Paperbacks

I FORGOT TO WEAR UNDERWEAR ON A GLASS-BOTTOM BOAT

ISBN: 0–312–96264–9

Printed in the United States of America

St. Martin's Paperbacks trade paperback edition/July 1997

10   9   8   7   6   5   4   3   2   1

Foreword

Warning! If you can't keep a secret, close this book now. (But not too fast. Yesterday, someone shut a copy on her ice-cream cone and had to pay for it anyway.)

Still here? Okay. Then lean back, relax, suck a breath mint, whatever.

You're probably as ready as you'll ever be for the fascinating secrets of ordinary Americans. Secrets like the one from the lawyer who's still trick-or-treating at age forty-five. Or the woman whose first orgasm put her in the emergency room.

In publishing a newsletter called *The Secrets Exchange*, we invite ordinary people across the country to tell us secrets they can't tell anyone else. To guarantee their privacy, we promise secret-tellers complete anonymity.

We sensed the need for such a publication after many years as freelance reporters for publications ranging from newspapers to supermarket tabloids. In more than 1,500 articles, we interviewed over 6,000 people, like the accountant who adds and subtracts on her fingers and toes and the country music singer who keeps a gerbil in his hat when he's onstage.

In the course of interviews, people often told us about family problems or personal hang-ups, secret dreams and desires—intimate revelations that had nothing to do with the story at hand. Why? We were easy to talk to, sympathetic voices on the other end of the phone, people they would never meet again and never have to worry about.

Which brings us to secrets. We realized that ordinary Americans needed an outlet for getting secrets off their chests. Very few can afford a shrink and most worry about their confession coming back to haunt them if they tell a friend. And, certainly, the vast majority don't want the exposure that would follow spilling their guts out on a TV talk show.

So we founded *The Secrets Exchange* newsletter—with the kitchen table as our "office." Through classified ads and word of mouth, we invited the public to send us their secrets. The mail has poured in ever since.

We receive letters from medical doctors, college students, business owners, and homemakers, people with advanced degrees and people who write with crayons.

Obviously, the desire to tell a secret is universal. What happens, then, if you hold it in? According to psychological studies, what you don't say can hurt you. Keeping secrets can lead to physical disorders, like headaches and high blood pressure. One university researcher found that 20 percent of his subjects had never confided their biggest secret to another human being. Surprisingly, most of these concerned embarrassing experiences, not painful incidents. Because not all secrets are deep and dark, the stuff contained in a horror novel or a call to Dr. Laura.

Our focus is on that lighter, brighter side of secrets. The embarrassing, awkward, highly personal but humorous moments we all experience but would never reveal publicly.

It's our daily privilege to review piles of eye-opening revelations from folks who may be your friends, neighbors, co-workers, or classmates.

We've pulled together the best from our files to share with you personally.

But before you read further, we ask that you raise your right hand and solemnly swear, "No matter how much I am tempted, I will not reveal these amazing secrets to another living soul. Especially if they haven't bought the book."

Contents

I forgot to wear underwear on a glass-bottom boat :

REAL PEOPLE, TRUE SECRETS

Chapter 1

Work

Shrink:
The Patient I Pay to Show Up

It was another one of *those* days. "If I hear one more whiner I'm going to scream. Haven't you people heard of a stiff upper lip?" I hissed in frustration as my latest crybaby patient disappeared through the door. "This is all *your* fault," I raged, throwing my mail at the poster of Freud hanging behind my desk.

Having vented, I became as placid and calm as a mountain lake, my professional veneer. I reflected that whiners are an occupational hazard for psychiatrists, just like litterbugs are to street sweepers. It's something you have to accept when you choose the gig. Trouble is, you don't learn you'll be spending your working life with the biggest complainers on earth until you've spent thousands and thousands of dollars and over a decade earning the sheepskin that brings you your doom.

Well, just one more patient today—and 287 working days until my Florida retirement.

The new client entered. "Jeff" I wrote in big block letters at the top of my legal pad. A frustrated comedian with low self-esteem because nobody liked his material. Too bad. He seemed like a nice kid, the nerd always a little out of touch.

"How'd your show go last night?" That should be good for ten minutes of kvetching.

"Bombed!" Jeff put his hands to his head and began to weep.

Uh-oh. Not a full session of blubbering! "Why don't you do your act for me?" I asked in desperation.

"I've only got forty minutes of material."

"Fine. That's all the time we have left."

Jeff proceeded to stand, smooth his madras sport coat, and keep me in stitches until my egg timer rang.

"Stop, stop," I pleaded, wiping away tears of joy.

"I've got a little more," Jeff replied. He was all pumped up.

"No, we'd go over. I'd have to charge more."

"I feel great!" Jeff yelped.

The boy had talent. I don't have space to go into it here, but if you ever hear the one about the priest, the rabbi, and the Mormon Tabernacle Choir in a rowboat, listen carefully. It's hysterical. Jeff had me feeling like I was watching *The Ed Sullivan Show*.

"See you next Thursday, same time," I said, still smiling.

Jeff frowned. "Uh, about that, doc. Low on funds. Can't come back. But thanks for hearing my show."

Inspiration struck. "Listen. Show up. It'll be on me. But you have to promise me something. Two weeks from now, I want you here with fifteen minutes of fresh material. And I'll pay *you*."

"You're on," Jeff enthused, clapping his hands.

Now, twice a month, Jeff tries out new material on me. I critique. He feels better. I feel better. And isn't that what therapy is all about?

The only difference here is *my* wallet is lighter.

Bad Boss Payback:
Revenge of the Sardines

I look like the kind of woman you can trust. At the mall, strangers leave their toddlers with me while they run to the restroom. People stop me on the street to ask for directions. That's why I get away with stuff that would hang somebody else, like the time I took revenge on my boss, the public relations director of a large computer company.

We nicknamed her "the Beast." Not only was she power-hungry and petty-minded, she was vindictive. In the four years I endured her, I saw her reduce people to tears with her terrible tongue-lashings, including me. Revenge was the only option.

One Sunday, I went to the office with a tin of sardines. I looked around carefully, making absolutely sure nobody else was there. I crouched behind the Beast's chair. Opening the sardine can, I placed the oily little fish in the short metal tray right under the seat. Then I left.

The next morning, I came in late and found the place in an uproar. The Beast was upset. She told everyone that something must have died in her office over the weekend. She had the building engineers take apart the ceiling tiles, the baseboards, her desk—even her computer. Everything but the chair!

Behind her back, the staff giggled and cracked jokes. Then the engineers gave up the quest. Nothing could be found.

Over the next couple of weeks, the Beast took to using other offices to do her work. She wore heavy perfume, as if she thought the pungent odor in her office had something to do with her personally. She even complained to me about the problem. I smiled sympathetically and asked, all innocence: "Have you had a physical lately? You might want to talk this over with your doctor. . . ."

Secret *Fortune* 500 Plan
to Franchise Lemonade Stands

Time was, you bought your groceries from a mom-and-pop store down the street. Today you shop at a gigantic supermarket where some kind of laser beam adds up your bill.

Big business is taking over everything. Now, not even my child's hopes and dreams are safe from the tentacles of greed.

"Laura" is an overactive nine-year-old who was slowly driving me nuts during our last summer vacation. I decided to channel her energies into a constructive activity that would also teach her the basics of our free enterprise system: a curbside lemonade stand.

Laura took to the idea with enthusiasm, especially when I promised to make the lemonade, set up the card table, paint the signs, crush the ice, and provide five dollars in change as seed money.

The first afternoon, she made seventy-five cents, excellent considering she and a friend drank the rest of her product. The following day, Laura's gross soared to two-fifty. By the end of the week she was raking in twenty dollars a day.

That's when the distinguished, silver-haired gentleman in the black Rolls bought his first large lemonade. I thought it was cute that he even chatted with Laura. But when he reappeared three times in as many days, I began to worry.

Worry turned to fear when I learned that he was pumping Laura for information. While some people may consider "How's business?" an innocent question, this mother's instinct said "Not!"

The next time he showed, I was ready in the family car. It seemed as though I had trailed that Rolls-Royce forever when it slipped quietly through the guarded gates of a huge national conglomerate.

I almost fainted. A multibillion-dollar company was conspiring to rip off Laura's successful formula for selling lemonade. Multiply twenty dollars a day by thousands of stands across the country and you don't have to guess why.

Since then, I drive the streets daily, looking for lemonade stands that are carbon copies of Laura's. If I ever find one, I'm suing the pants off that copycat company!

I Spent an Entire Day
Working for the Wrong Company

Impossible, you say? Well, what if you're really, really sleepy and, okay, hung over?

It's not because I'm stupid. I moved to this major metropolitan center to take art classes and support myself doing office work. Luckily, I found a reliable temporary employment agency.

My first assignment seemed easy enough: receptionist duties for a high-level corporate executive. The agency's "employment counselor" filled out a form and told me to present it to the supervising secretary in the department. The job was to start the next day.

That evening, my new roommate threw a sedate dinner party that turned into an all-night rave.

The morning arrived as a throbbing-brain blur. I changed out of my party dress and stumbled to the bus stop, hoping I wouldn't be "tardy" for work. In the course of all this frenetic activity, I somehow managed to lose the slip which my employment counselor had handed me. Panic!

I had barely glanced at the paper and recalled only vaguely the name and address of the firm—something to do with insurance, marble-and-brick tower fronted by a spectacular sculpture garden, eighth floor. . . .

Found the building, the elevator, the floor. "You're late," snapped the tall, silk-suited brunette who cornered me as I walked through the door. "I don't have time to explain things," she said, as she hustled me into a quiet office. "Just answer the phone and take messages." She vanished.

I slipped into my own hungover world, answered calls in a fake cheery voice, then left for the day at 5:30, a pile of forty-eight neatly completed message slips sitting on the desk.

That night at home the phone rang. "Where were you today?" asked the woman from the temp agency. "The company says you never showed up."

Oh, my God! How could I possibly explain?

"Would you believe I picked the wrong building?" I asked.

"No," she said.

"Do I get paid anyway?"

"Nice try," she sniffed, just before the line went dead.

Former Male Stripper:
My Career-Killing Boner
(Sorry, boys, this secret is "ladies only." Men can return after this page.)

I guess you could call me a poster boy for priapism. But I don't consider myself a charity case. I haven't even applied for disability yet, although I think there's a fighting chance I could get it.

I'm still buff. I could hop on stage right now and provide you delicious ladies with a solid hour of boffo entertainment. The hangup is, I've got a "woodie" that won't quit.

I'm a pariah in my chosen profession, all because of a single fateful encounter. I was playing a seminaked fireman when I slipped on some body oil and fell into the audience. Upending several horny babes in the process, I came to rest face-first in a shot glass, raising a huge welt on my forehead. Unfortunately, it also began to raise a lower, more embarrassing part of my anatomy.

Trooper that I am, I tried to complete my show, but my still-rising member soon had every lady around me screaming. I wasn't offended. I understand how you can experience an over-reaction when you come face to face with a stranger's boner at a bachelorette party.

I raced offstage and thought my nightmare was over. It was only beginning. I developed some sort of "complex" due to the trauma of my accident. Every time I tried to dance I'd pull a Pinocchio. Now I can't even go near a strip club without wearing baggy pants and a raincoat. I've tried every remedy. So far, nothing has worked.

But don't get ready to put this stud out to pasture yet. I'll consult every medical expert in the country before I hang up the old G-string.

Soon enough I'll be catching your dollar bills in my butt cheeks, which is a new trick I've been practicing at home.

Fired, Then Rehired, Under a Different Name

I never expected to set the world on fire when I took my first job. I just wanted to be able to pay the rent, put gas in the car, and have enough money left over for a bottle of wine at the end of the week, so I became a paper shuffler at a huge financial institution.

Sure, I was bored, but the benefits were great and my coworkers were terrific. We all shared the same relaxed attitude: The work would get done, we just didn't know when.

Things changed abruptly when our unit got a new boss. His sole purpose, he announced at a meeting, was to put our department on the map. He exhorted us to "climb aboard for an exciting ride to the top."

Where are we going, I wondered, to Paris and the Eiffel Tower? I let out a little guffaw, immediately trying to cover it with a cough. No luck. He glared my way.

From that moment on, his mission in life was to get rid of me—and he did. Within weeks, he had catalogued enough of my sins to justify a pink slip.

After collecting unemployment benefits for six months, I reluctantly began looking for work. But nothing met my criterion: they all seemed like real jobs. I began to daydream about the two-hour coffee breaks and "no-work Fridays" of my previous gig. Then I picked up the Sunday paper and a thrill went down my spine. My previous employer had job openings.

This was too good to pass up: a paycheck for moving piles of paper from one desk to another. All I had to do was avoid my former boss. I changed my hairstyle, going from brown to honey-blond, and I bought a new outfit in a style I never wore. When I looked in the mirror, I didn't recognize myself.

At the interview I used my maiden name so they wouldn't find a file on me. My résumé noted that I had spent the last three years working in Italy. Nobody knew how to speak Italian so they didn't try to check.

I was hired a week later. I now work for another department three floors up from my previous one. I'm careful to avoid that area, but none of my previous coworkers recognize me anyway.

The funny thing is I was hired for twice my previous salary and was just voted Employee of the Month.

Busted! For an After-Sex Cigarette in a Nonsmoking Motel Room

I'm usually a pipe man myself, as befits a tenured professor of my standing. Oh, to contemplate sweet tendrils of smoke as they waft towards the ceiling. Such ethereal shapes ease the burden of grading Creative Writing 101 students. Some I give "A," others "F." I cannot explain why, other than I am impulsive by nature.

Yes, the law of the jungle applies to academia too, as has been the theme of all my novellas, which one day will be published, shall justice be served.

This primitive aspect of man also applies to sexual relationships, even those that transpire in the classroom setting. Case in point: my affair with "Sarah," a ravishing student a generation my junior. Some might be shocked by our tryst, surely my wife, but what is twenty years in the grand scheme of things? The blink of an eye.

Not surprisingly, considering the subject of this essay, it was tobacco that brought us together and tobacco that rent us asunder. For Sarah, I believe, fell in lust with my pipe, while I found the Virginia Slims betwixt her slender, painted fingers stimulating in the extreme.

Frankly, I consider the best fiction to be drawn from the author's own life experience. And grading papers is no kind of experience at all, which is why I whisked Sarah away in my 1963 Corvette Stingray for a few days alone. There was a book in it somewhere. Or at least a short story under a nom de plume.

I can't say Sarah was one of my premiere students—in truth, she was one of the worst. Yet, in keeping with my notion that experience is essential to fiction writers, I knew that after this weekend I could give her nothing but an "A." Perhaps years from now her liaison with the "old professor" would stimulate her creative juices and a wonderful new novelist would be born. At least, that was what I hoped.

It was with consternation that we found the out-of-the-way motel was entirely booked. Dismay turned to joy as a cancellation was phoned in—albeit for a nonsmoking room.

Sarah was a chain smoker. I, of course, enjoyed my pipe, so it was a big sacrifice for us to assume nonsmoking quarters. Sarah, as youth would have it, lost control first. I found her on her knees in the bathroom, blowing smoke down the toilet, with the hope that it would be sucked away as she flushed. This so endeared Sarah to me that I could not help but embrace her. One thing led to another and forty-five minutes later we were relaxing in our rumpled bed, engaging in postcoital chitchat.

"Professor, do you mind if I light up?" Sarah asked, suggestively drawing a slender cigarette from her pack.

Carefree, I replied, "My dear, I'll have one myself." We spent the next few minutes puffing dreamily in the great movie tradition.

Then our quiet reverie was interrupted by an insistent knock at the door. "Management," a voice grunted. "You're smoking in a nonsmoking room. May we come in?"

I bolted from bed and quickly raised the windows. "Just a moment," I pleaded. To no avail. Sarah, the maddening naif, had already opened the door.

The manager and a security guard entered, catching me in a frieze of ashes, cigarette smoke, and nudity.

Fifteen minutes later, Sarah and I were back in my 'vette. The atmosphere? Chilly.

Sarah and I never spoke again, although I felt she still deserved the top grade.

I continue to write, though I prefer to expend my creative energies on my most promising students.

Veteran Accountant:
I Add and Subtract on My Fingers and Toes

I have some big-money clients and they'd burp a brick if they knew the truth about this tax gal. I count so much with my fingers and toes that around April 15th I sprout blisters like popcorn. I wear Band-Aids everywhere and just grit my teeth until the last 1040 goes out the door.

It's been this way for decades, ever since I learned this method as a lass. Since then, I've become quite prosperous and have learned many sophisticated ways. I know fine wines and can even eat snails with a smile. But when I go back to the office, it's off with my wedding ring, hose, and patent leather pumps. I lean back in my leather chair, sprinkle talcum on my appendages, and go back to counting the old-fashioned way.

Some of my fellow accountants tell me they'll know it's time to quit when their mind starts to go. But my biggest fear is arthritis. When my hands and feet get too painful to move, I'll know it's time to pack up the ledgers and call it a day.

One fringe benefit of my secret habit: all that exercise has given me the grip of a lobster; you couldn't pry a buck out of my hands with a chisel.

Chapter 2

Love and Sex

The Only Way We Can Get Ready for Romance Is to Do the Twist

For some people, it's flowers and a gourmet dinner in the best restaurant in town. For us, dancing the Twist unlocks the door to romance!

My husband and I are baby boomers who met as teens in high school. We did all the fun things kids did back in the '60s—sock hops, midnight movies, and endless cruising.

Our absolute favorite activity, though, was dancing at parties. We'd turn the lights low and slow-dance for hours. But one night our pals introduced us to a brand new sound—Chubby Checker's version of the Twist. It hooked us! We spent hours mastering the art of the Twist, even practicing in front of a full-length mirror to get our moves down. Our friends really admired our style.

It was during this time that we fell in love and made plans for marriage after our high school graduation. We exchanged vows when we were both just nineteen. Then married life began for real: four babies all in a row, a husband who was establishing his own business and plenty of money worries.

Without wanting it to happen, passion took a backseat to the pressures of everyday life. Although we still adored each other, we somehow lost the sexy bond that keeps a man and woman together. That is, until the day we heard the Twist again—after twenty-five long years. A radio station was playing the song as we were driving home from the kids' track meet.

My heart suddenly skipped a beat. The music stirred up emotions that I thought had long since died. I glanced over at my husband and saw his eyes light up with love.

When we got home, we Twisted our way to the bedroom— and the most wonderful night of passion we've ever known.

Since then, whenever we want to set the mood for love, we turn the lights down low—and turn on with the Twist!

No Shirt, No Shoes, No Sex

I'm a loose woman. I do not discriminate against men by race, creed, color, or hat size. It is important in this day and age to support diversity, for that is our country's future. It's the least I can do—go out with any guy, whether he's bald, fat, from Alabama, or has some other kind of thing wrong with him.

Whoa, there! Before you start thinking I'm some kind of honky-tonk Mother Teresa, I have a confession to make. I do have my standards.

Here's the place where I draw a line in the sand: no shirt, no shoes, no sex.

Let me give you an example: One night in the bar where I work, a biker sauntered in. What a load! His beer belly was covered with hair so thick pieces of food stuck to it. His ape arms were black with tattoos, and his blue jeans smelled like an animal shelter. But I let him stay. Why? He wore a black leather vest. It finished the look. We even became an item until the end of the week, when he broke probation on a technical matter.

On the other hand, a hunk strode in once looking fine as could be, a combination of the best qualities of Brad Pitt and Mel Gibson. Unfortunately, he was barefoot and his torso was devoid of a stitch. Then he came on to me before even buying a beer. Not only did he not get my number, I had the bouncer throw him out of the place.

My heart skipped a beat as his beautiful body whistled through the door. I even felt bad about him stumbling around barefoot in the cold night wearing only cutoffs. But my better sense won out and I didn't budge from my stool.

To this day, our regulars believe I was trying to keep riffraff out of the joint. It goes deeper than that. I was trying to keep it out of my bed.

Still, I think of "Brad Gibson" often and his hard bod hurtling into that snowbank. Some uptown watering holes keep a tie and sport coat handy for men not properly dressed by their standards. Maybe I should keep a spare sweatshirt and tennis shoes by our door, so I don't have to compromise my principles and let another good one stagger away in the night.

Fitness Nut's Secret "Intercourse Workout"

Whew! Gotta catch my breath. Just had sex with my boyfriend and I'm feeling the burn. Not from intercourse, silly, but from the workout I engaged in while I was between the sheets. Yes, I've found you can tone the old bod and burn extra calories just by pepping up your sex life.

The good news is your partner doesn't even have to know about it. You'll simply appear as an especially enthusiastic sex partner. Nothing wrong with that. All it takes is your willingness to forego the pleasure of the moment and keep your mind on the business at hand: a heart-pumping twenty-minute aerobic routine.

The key is to work out every part of your body, not just those below the waist. This way, you utilize twice the calories for double the benefits. For example, I don't allow my arms to cling passively to my lover. Instead, I do a series of arm lifts using small dumbbells, if available.

When we switch positions and I'm on top, I take the opportunity to do push-ups. It's easy: bend forward from the waist and try for ten in a row. I've advanced enough to try the one-handed version.

Will your partner notice, you ask? Probably not. I find that once properly motivated toward his goal, a male having sex likes to stay focused. He may not wonder, or care much, what you're doing. Therefore, you're pretty much free to go about your routine without any interference from him.

In fact, if you're like me, you may start thinking of your man as just another piece of exercise equipment.

I Wear a Surgical Mask When I Make Love

Boy, do I hate germs. Maybe it's because I study bacteria all day long as a lab technician. It's gotten to where I can actually feel the little devils crawling all over me—ugh.

Before you think I've gone overboard, digest these statistics I came up with:

- If germs were the size of dimes, they'd cover every square inch of the planet and we wouldn't be able to move.
- If you laid every germ in Kentucky end to end, you'd have a string of filth from here to the sun.

As you might imagine, at home I'm a one-woman war machine against all manner of loathsome organisms. As I like to say: germs never sleep and they don't take vacations.

Procter & Gamble should honor my name, God knows, since I single-handedly support them. I have enough disinfectants, cleansers, sprays, scrubbing gels, mops, sponges, and wipes to clean up every Boy Scout camp in America. Another statistic: Cub Scouts sport 350 percent more germs than Brownies after eating S'mores.

I thought I had every germ in my life under control, until I read the human mouth is the filthiest place on earth. This really freaked me, as you can't gargle with Lysol.

The problem is I live with my boyfriend and he's always trying to kiss me at the height of passion. But when I brought up the problem of the human mouth, he started to get up-tight. We decided to compromise: he'd let me wear the surgical mask when we French-kissed if I stopped boiling his bubble gum before he chewed it. That's fair.

One final statistic: If boyfriends were germs, you'd be dating thousands of them at a time.

"I'm with 32A": Boyfriend's Secret T-Shirt Has Her Fuming

Okay, so I'm flat-chested, but does he have to rub it in? I love him, but the guy's about as subtle as mud-wrestling.

"Buddy" used to ride me all the time about being flat. I mean he'd salivate so much when *Baywatch* came on TV that he needed a bib. I can't tell you how embarrassing it is to have your boyfriend point to a starlet on the screen and pant, "That one. Get breasts like her," especially at a family reunion.

We had some mighty battles, that boy and me, but I finally laid down the law: if he said another word about big boobs, I was outta there. I could see that scared him and for about six weeks I had peace. I even did some research, finding that some of the great women in history were flat-chested. Joan of Arc, Annie Oakley, and Mata Hari all had fried-egg breasts—at least that's how they looked in books.

But last week Buddy staged a sneak attack. While barbecuing chicken with our friends, he unzipped his bomber jacket to reveal a T-shirt with writing below. It read: "I'M WITH 32A." The visual was a pair of deflated balloons. I snapped it shut before anyone could see it.

"You promised," I hissed between clenched teeth.

"You said I couldn't say a word. Nothing about writing," he answered with a big, manure-eating grin.

Friday at the mall, I figured out how to get even.

That night I went to a party with Buddy. After hanging my coat in the closet, I strode into the living room, wearing my new custom-made top. It was a T-shirt featuring a comment on the state of Buddy's masculinity: "I'M WITH 3 INCHES." There was a very short cigar butt beneath. Everybody in the room began to howl. Buddy's face turned crimson red.

The past couple of days, he's been strangely silent on the subject of breasts. He even bought me a bouquet of orchids. I have the T-shirt folded in my bureau; it guarantees to keep him on such good behavior.

I Made My Hubby Lose Twenty-Five Pounds— Now Beer Bellies Turn Me On

When my husband and I married ten years ago, we were seriously into fitness. Once I got an eyeful of him in running shorts and tank top, it was lust at first sight.

We kept up our workouts after marriage, but suddenly all that went out the window for "Don" when he got a new job. Don began working day and night, coming home from the office too stressed to talk. For the first time in his life, he began eating more and giving up his workouts to do paperwork at home. Within a year, his weight ballooned up twenty-five pounds!

I begged, nagged, and cajoled Don to go on a diet. I wanted my old husband back, the lean, muscular man I'd married years before. Frankly, none of my whining had any effect on him at all until I hinted strongly that his new "pleasingly plump" physique was less than pleasing in the bedroom department.

That did it! He gave up desserts, ate no more than 1,000 calories daily, and went to the gym regularly. Slowly, the pounds started melting away and Don began looking like his old self again: lean, hard, and fit. I should have been thrilled, but I wasn't. A bizarre change was coming over me. Oversized, hefty guys started looking mighty good—guys who seemed like big, rumpled teddy bears just waiting for a hug.

Incredibly, the thinner Don became, the more I found myself gazing at love handles and beer bellies. Ordinary men as big and comfy as the old couch in your living room began turning me on. I couldn't tell you in a million years why. Of course, after the fuss I made about his extra pounds, how could I tell Don to put back the weight?

I've taken to hanging around places where guys don't seem to care about their waistlines, like pool halls and bowling alleys. At least I can look.

Marriage Made Me a Hit With Men

I was a drip in high school. A loser. Sure, I was smart, college-bound, and aimed for success. But what I wanted most—a date with a hunk—evaded me.

Looking back, I was cute in a tomboyish kind of way. That is, I tried to look hip and "interesting" because there was no way I would have been called beautiful. A prom queen I wasn't. Still, I don't think it was my looks that turned off men. My girlfriends said it was my attitude. They said I didn't know how to talk to guys, or flirt with them, or seduce them into wanting me. They gave me all sorts of advice, but none of it worked.

I went to business school and met a guy in one of my classes. "T" and I became fast friends, even did our homework together. That's why when he asked me out, I didn't even consider it a date. Not long after that first get-together, we fell in love and got married.

Marriage worked wonders for me. It was like I was emitting a hormone that drew men into my force field. Once I had to use a bus when my car broke down. I was sitting there minding my own business when a young guy rushed up and stuck a wadded-up note into my hand. It read, "You're fabulous. I've fallen in love with you." I never saw him again.

But that's nothing compared to the guy at the grocery store who wanted to make lasagna for me—with his homemade pasta, for God's sake! Or, the man at the cleaner's who wanted to show me his ironing technique. Or, the myriad guys at work, on the street, at my fitness club who try, sometimes desperately, sometimes endearingly, to get close to me. Some of them leave messages on my phone machine, others just happen to bump into me in the lunch line.

Now that I'm a happily married woman, I'm finally popular with men. Funny thing, I'm not even tempted.

I just have one question for all my admirers: Where were you when I needed you?

My First Orgasm
Sent Me to the Emergency Room

Most girls think they've died and gone to heaven when they first experience it. I just thought I'd died.

I'll admit I've always been somewhat anxious. When I was just eight, I focused on blinking. I worried that I'd go blind if I didn't blink on a regular basis, so I began counting each one. I stopped at 8,293 when my Dad shouted that if I didn't quit it, he'd tape my eyes shut.

By ten, I'd graduated to *Reader's Digest*. Whatever disease they featured each issue, I'd come down with it. The article on leprosy put me through hell for a month. It was a relief when the next issue appeared, featuring chronic heartburn.

This brings me to 1965, when I was fifteen. "Orville," my then boyfriend, and I were in the backseat of his Dad's Buick Electra, doing what was called "heavy petting." I was nervous. I wanted to impress him; his father was a dermatologist.

Orville was exceptionally enthusiastic this particular evening. His hands roamed all over, then focused on a particular spot. An odd sensation began in the vicinity of my stomach and soon engulfed my whole body.

Fear, then panic, took over as my body convulsed rhythmically. I screamed.

"Darling," Orville sighed.

"Take me to the emergency room. I'm dying," I hollered, gasping for air.

"Could you wait half a minute?" Orville grunted.

Twenty minutes later I was dressed in a hospital gown, having a quiet chat with the kindly resident doctor, while two older nurses watched and smirked.

"You're perfectly fine," said the doctor. "I think what you experienced was a simply a sexual climax, called an orgasm. You know what that is, don't you?"

I assured him I did, trying to seem mature and sophisticated about such things. But my sex advisor, my fourteen-year-old best friend, had never informed me about such an event.

As for Orville, we broke up. He said I was a little too "high-strung."

I Waited Sixty Years for the Girl of My Dreams: It Wasn't Worth It

A famous man once said good things come to those who wait. Boy, was that egghead full of it! I spent six decades pining for my true love's hand. But then I carried her over the threshold and it's been downhill ever since.

Here's how this so-called love story started. I was the star halfback on my high school football team in Los Angeles. "Muriel" was the head cheerleader. I asked her to the Junior Prom. We danced until midnight and kissed only once. From that day forward I could never get her out of my mind. Apparently, Muriel didn't feel the same, because she married the team's waterboy straight out of school.

The years flew by. I was never able to develop a lasting relationship with a lady because every time I was about to kiss one, I saw Muriel's face and felt guilty. Then fate intervened. Early this year I was lifting weights at Muscle Beach in Venice, California, when I spotted a familiar, if aged, face: it was Muriel's.

My heart pounded in my chest as I jogged over to greet her, a dumbbell in each hand. Though older, she was as classy as ever—sort of like a used Cadillac in need of bodywork. But at seventy-eight, aren't we all? We hit it off right away. Not only that, the waterboy was history. I was within reach of my life-long goal.

Three months ago, we married. That should have been the final chapter of a storybook romance. But while one dream was ending, a nightmare was beginning. Muriel has more bad habits than Mother Teresa.

Where should I start? Just to give you a hint, she still calls Jay Leno "Johnny" and can't wait for the next Clark Gable picture. Every time we go dancing, she insists on wearing her Veronica Lake wig.

I envy Romeo. He had the good luck to drop dead as a kid— before he discovered the "real" Juliet wore hair rollers and needed more fiber.

Chapter 3

Pets

I Only Had Kids
Because I'm Allergic to Fur

Ever since I can first remember, my passion has been pets. The furrier the better. Persian cats, tiny Lhasa Apso dogs—I love them all. Put me in a room with a bouncing ball of fur and before you can blink, she'll be in my arms getting the best and warmest cuddle that little 'un ever had. Not only that, I'll tie satin ribbons and bows to her mounds of fur to make her even cuter. A spray of cologne on the tail (hers), a dab behind the ears (mine), and that sassy lady and me are ready for all comers.

The hitch is that after a day of such joy, I'm screaming for dear life in the emergency room, with a pulsating case of hives from head to toe.

I found I was allergic to fur when I was but five. Mother rushed me to the doctor, my body covered with so many red and purple blisters he said I looked like a "technicolor toad." My parents were forced to get rid of my precious Persian kitten.

How I have suffered since! Do you know what it's like to go thirty-seven years longing for the touch of fur? To break out in horrifying, festering pain if you "go off the wagon" and pet the little darling who curls against your leg on your evening stroll? I have spent my entire life behind an invisible barrier, unable to hug the living creatures I hold most dear.

My own children do not receive such love. They are three of the finest kids a mom could want. But they are not what I desire. I have never told this to anyone, but the first toy each baby got was a darling catnip mouse. I just couldn't resist.

This secret will be lowered with me into the grave, unless science allows me to feel once more the pleasure of fur.

Catnip Leaves Kitty Cold, But Gets Owner Sky-High

I'm a twenty-nine-year-old secretary who's crazy about her cat. Annabelle (not her real name) has been with me for thirteen years and she still behaves like a kitten. Although I adore Annabelle, I know she's not too bright. I've had to teach her things most felines seem to know instinctively, like how to chase squirrels or wash her face.

Luckily, Annabelle has been a dutiful student. If she needs to learn something, I set her down and just show her what she's supposed to do. Like drinking milk, for example. I got down on all fours and lapped from the bowl. After that, she got the hang of it.

Not long ago, Annabelle seemed to be in a funk. She'd stare out of the window for hours on end, eat a little chopped turkey and giblets, lick herself, and fall asleep for the rest of the day. Not much of a life, I thought! That's when I decided to buy some catnip to perk her up a bit. While I've never been a believer in artificial stimulants for her (or me!), I thought an innocent herb like catnip shouldn't present any problems.

I bought some fresh catnip at my pet store and arranged it nicely in a dish. Annabelle didn't seem inclined to inspect the bowl, so I got down on my hands and knees to show her what to do. I placed my head directly over the dish and took a whiff of the weedy stuff. Annabelle seemed bored. I turned back to the bowl and sniffed again, hoping to arouse her interest. Within a few seconds, I was amazed to find myself feeling utterly and completely relaxed, deliciously euphoric, free of worry and anxiety. It was akin to floating on a cloud in a blue summer sky, a perfect moment.

Annabelle turned up her nose at the catnip and went back to her window perch to watch an ant. I, on the other hand, took another whiff and experienced bliss. I sprawled on my back on the kitchen floor, convinced Annabelle didn't know what she was missing.

Now, whenever I'm tense, I stick my head in a bowl of catnip and just escape for a few minutes. I think I have more feline in me than my own cat.

Ten-Gallon Country Hunk:
I Keep a Gerbil in My Hat
When I'm Playing Onstage . . .

Other people have a lucky rabbit's foot, but I have a lucky gerbil. His name is Buster and he's been with me since I signed my recording contract. I was celebrating with a buying spree at the local mall when I hurried by one of those pet stores they have there.

There were a bunch of baby gerbils in the window. Most of them were huddled together and sleeping, but one little old guy was trying to scratch his way through the glass. I knew instantly we were brothers under the skin: both of us lone wolves and scrappers, bound and determined to claw our way out of the rat race. And I already had a name for him—Buster—after my dear, departed Dad.

I paid the clerk. My arms were so full of packages, I just had her shove Buster under my hat. The rest is history. As I left the mall, I could feel him gently scratching out a nest for himself in my hair, after which he instantly fell asleep.

We've been inseparable ever since. As I have struggled for my fair share of riches and fame, Buster has struggled with me. We've crisscrossed this wonderful country of ours many times and have made some of the best fans in the world. I've even taken him on some of my dates. (The girls never knew he was there. I *always* keep my hat on, if you catch my drift.)

We do need some time apart, so at home I built Buster a scale model of my barn, complete with his own miniature gold records. I only hope that one day I have as many real ones.

Buster's a born ham and he's happiest when we're entertaining a screaming crowd. He raises quite a ruckus during our fast numbers. I call his footwork the "Gerbil Two-step." He naps during our acoustic set.

Our scariest time together was when we were alone offstage at a county fair. A strong wind blew my hat off and Buster hit the ground running for the Small Animal Hall. I guess he wanted to engage in a little "meet and greet" at the gerbil exhibit. I dove headfirst into the sawdust and caught him an eye blink before he disappeared.

Critics claim I keep my hat on 'cause I'm going bald. I'm willing to take the heat. I know Buster would if he were in my position.

It hurts to think of it, but Buster's getting up there in gerbil years. When he passes into the Great Beyond, I'm either going to have him stuffed or turn him into a coin purse so he can be with me always.

Hey, do me a favor. Next time one of us "hat acts" hops onstage—say hello to Buster!

I Trained My Neighbor's Dog
to Annoy Him

"Rover" is a highly intelligent black Labrador who responds well to human commands. I once taught an award-winning dog obedience class at our community college. Together we make a wonderful team.

Rover and I met when his obnoxious, foul-mouthed owner moved in next door, spoiling the serenity of my retirement years. I guess "Hal" is what they call a yuppie, though even those rude egocentrics would probably find him a pain in the ass. For instance:

- His favorite place for a phone conversation is on a cordless phone in the backyard. His favorite volume is at the top of his lungs.
- He owns four snowmobiles and turns his one-acre lot into a wintertime racetrack for himself, his wife, and two sons. The exhaust fumes get you if the noise doesn't.
- His boys celebrate the Fourth of July with firecrackers and Roman candles from the time summer vacation starts until Labor Day.
- The wife spends hours a day with her "personal trainer," dancing and prancing to loud aerobic music.

Of the entire brood, only Rover shows any human decency. Like most dogs, he's naturally gregarious and giving. If you scratch Rover's back, he'll look for a way to scratch yours. I took advantage of this trait by offering Rover a lot of love and a few free training lessons. Soon, Rover was responding to a variety of commands. All it took was the right number of toots from my supersonic dog whistle.

These days, Rover and I love to play "fetch." In fact, a few weeks ago he fetched Hal's cordless telephone and buried it deep in the garden. Poor Hal never did find it.

Rover also enjoys tracking scent. One afternoon, he retrieved the personal trainer's Calvin Klein briefs from the bedroom, then brought them to Hal along with the evening paper. That was the last time I saw the personal trainer or heard the aerobic music.

A dog is man's best friend. Which man depends on how well you scratch his back.

Soft-Hearted Angler:
I Catch All My Fish at the Supermarket

I look like I belong in the great outdoors—a guy who lives to fish and hunt. I'm naturally muscular, shop at "big & tall" stores, and seem most comfortable in a plaid flannel shirt and work boots. Appearances, however, are deceptive.

I'm really something of a wimp. Case in point: the wife thinks I'm a crackerjack fisherman, that I'm out on the water by dawn to nail some sleepy-eyed perch before they're awake. The truth is I'm actually squeamish about fishhooks and blood—and I feel like crying when I see a fish gasping for air.

What I enjoy is just sitting on the boat drinking beer and listening to a ball game. I haven't touched a rod and reel in years. Every hour or so, I feed the fish with some pet store fish food. I sprinkle the stuff on the water, then watch in fascination as the perch and crappies nip at it from below. I just enjoy the show.

Of course, I can't tell my spouse the truth. If she knew I wasn't really fishing, she'd nag me to stay home and clean out the garage or take her and the kids to the mall. I love my family, but a guy needs a day to himself every now and then.

So what I do is stop at the market on the way home and pick up something that resembles freshwater fish. My wife only questioned me once—the time I brought home tuna fillets. I spent the whole evening convincing her that an entire species of tuna live in lakes.

I Only Stay with My Spouse
for the Sake of the Cats

There's nothing I wouldn't do for my three precious felines. And if that means staying in my crummy marriage while they live out their natural life span, so be it. It's a small price to pay for their happiness.

Mel, Jasmine, and Barry are three, five, and six, respectively. That means I face at least ten years' "hard time" in the custody of my warden, my wife. But I'm willing to sacrifice years of my life so that my cats can enjoy theirs.

It just so happens that my mate, who is a real firebreather with me, is a marvelous mother to our furry brood. She's up at first light, preparing them a fried kidney breakfast from scratch, straightening their beds, and getting them ready for the day ahead. While I'm at work, she's busy looking after them, and they truly adore her. I must give the warden credit where credit is due.

I could kidnap Mel, Jasmine, and Barry, but what sort of life would the three of them have, on the run from one cheap motel to another? I'd have to stop calling them by their real names. Maybe even dye their fur.

And divorce? The idea of destroying their contentment, their sense of peace and harmony in the world, by breaking up their happy home makes my blood run cold. How lonely and bereft they'd feel! Who'd get to keep the favorite scratching post? The homegrown catnip? I hate to think of the psychological damage to their tender psyches.

I accept my marital fate in silence and secrecy. The only thing I ask of my wife is that she refrain from calling me names in front of the cats. I don't want them to lose respect for me.

To Win the Man She Wooed the Dog

When I first saw the man of my dreams, I said a little prayer to myself: "Dear God, let him not be married, gay, or criminally insane."

God was kind. It turned out that "Doug" was just terminally shy and particularly wary of aggressive females looking for love. I guess I qualified. I'd just maxed out my credit card on personals ads.

Doug was a new neighbor who lived down the street in a pretty condo. He walked his sweet-faced golden retriever every day at about the same time, usually when I was returning from work. Unfortunately, Doug and I had trouble getting past "Hi." He obviously adored his dog Lana and seemed preoccupied by her well-being—for example, dressing her in a raincoat when the weather turned drizzly. I figured the only way to Doug's heart was through Lana. I dubbed my campaign "Love Doggy Style."

I started by giving Lana small treats when I ran into her and her owner: a small rubber ball, a meaty bone I picked out at a gourmet butcher shop, a stylish mohair sweater. Soon she began to view me as a friend, wagging her tail excitedly as I approached. After a few weeks of this, Lana was straining against her leash the instant she saw me.

I pretended to be surprised when Doug asked me over—alone. My heart thumped in my chest as we settled into his living room for coffee, just a hop, skip, and a jump from the bedroom. I cranked up erotic fantasies of Doug and me, with Lana asleep at the foot of the waterbed. What a fool, I, the Master Manipulator, turned out to be.

"I'm sorry," Doug said, his limpid blue eyes tearing, "I think Lana's crazy about you and I'm worried about losing her affection, but I'm a fighter. I'm going to walk her on a new route from now on and I'd appreciate it if you wouldn't follow us anymore. I know the breakup is going to be hard on you both, but no one ever said love was easy."

That night I cleared my cupboards of Alpo and went to a singles bar. Fortunately, there wasn't a dog in the place.

Chapter 4

Women

I Broke Wind and Scared a Burglar Away

I'm an elderly widow living in what was once a lovely part of Los Angeles. The late Mister and I used to take long walks at night without a care in the world. Locking doors was optional, and our two young boys would often "camp out" in the yard during summer. Today crime is high. I venture from my apartment only to shop and do laundry. I have three deadbolts on the door and the only people in the yard are winos and prowlers.

But I keep myself busy, so don't feel sorry for me. My boys don't, so why should you? They have better things to do, like get married, divorced, married, divorced. They're like a couple of Ping-Pong balls. You need a scorecard. And work? They're just waiting for their inheritance so they can live like bums for a couple more years.

Oh well, we all have our little flaws, don't we? And at forty-eight and fifty-one, they're still finding themselves. One even has a great future ahead of him when he graduates from college. Actually, they're the real reason I want to go on living as long as I can. That's why I pay attention to what I eat, especially fiber. I believe a cleansing diet of beans, fruit, bran, raisins, Metamucil, etc., keeps an older person alive longer if they stick to it, like I do.

A typical breakfast for me is Raisin Bran, whole-wheat toast, and a banana. Lunch is a small can of lima beans or meatless chili and Jell-O topped with crushed raw filberts. For supper, I usually savor a bowl of five-bean salad followed by celery sticks and a luscious dessert of room-temperature prunes. Then I sip on a glass of flavored Metamucil while enjoying an evening of my favorite "must-see" programs. (I firmly believe that my friends in the "fiber family" will add forty years to my life. My grieving boys won't lay me to rest until I'm a hundred and twenty-one—and they're eighty-eight and ninety-one.)

I was viewing the third hour of *Action News* one evening when I was startled by a scraping noise beneath the window. Figuring it was just a street person looking for a place to sleep, I rose to turn on the floodlight my landlady had installed.

It was then I received the fright of my life. A rock smashed through the window, followed by a hairy arm trying to work the latch.

"Go away!" I shouted, but my old lady's voice didn't stop him at all. I was beside myself with fear.

Now comes the embarrassing part, why I haven't been able to tell anyone my story. As you might imagine, my diet causes a lot of gas. Usually, I am well able to censure myself so that air comes out . . . silently. This time it emerged without warning, in three loud bangs that made me jump. The burglar's hairy arm withdrew in a flash, followed by the sound of breaking branches as he ran away. Apparently, the pistol-like reports I released made him think I had a gun.

It took me a month of Sundays to recover. Eventually, I saw

it as just one more benefit of fiber. Still, I could never bear to "go public" with my finding, even if it would help other elderly folks like me. Maybe I'll just pin a note to the Laundromat bulletin board when nobody else is there. Yes, that's what I'll do.

The Case of the Socialite Waitress

Last summer, I found myself hanging around cafés, sipping coffee, and gazing at dirty tables, fighting the overwhelming urge to make them spick-and-span. I itched to jump from my stool, wipe a wet cloth across the table, and rush the used dishes into the kitchen. Looking at the half-eaten plates of food with congealed gravy and fatty globs of mystery meat made me nauseous.

Finally, I couldn't hold myself back any longer. I found a coffee shop in another part of town where the waitresses were incredibly busy. Tables were piled high with dirty dishes, glasses, and silverware.

Wearing a clean white shirt and black skirt, like the regular help, I came back the next day during the lunch rush. Acting like I was supposed to be there, I walked right up to a table and began clearing down. The couple was so focused on their conversation they barely noticed me. As soon as my hands were full of dishes, I was off to the kitchen, dumping the load into the sink. The kitchen staff didn't even glance my way. Then I ran out the back door, nearly in a panic.

It all happened so quickly. But when it was over, I felt a sudden giddy rush of excitement plus a great sense of relief. Since that first unforgettable experience, I've been a "guerilla waitress" dozens of times. I case a place, hit it once, and vanish.

If you wonder why I don't get a restaurant job, here's the answer: my husband is a prominent businessman in our city; he thinks a man in his position shouldn't have a working wife. On top of that, we have a maid who cooks and cleans at home. This is why I have to satisfy my urges with other people's dirty dishes.

My Wedding Band Was a Mood Ring

Imagine: It's your wedding, the happiest day of your life. With tears rolling down your cheeks, you say, "I do," and your beloved new husband slips the ring on your finger. But instead of the diamond band you've been promised, it's an old mood ring handed down from his hippie mom.

This happened to me.

In fact, the only thing that saved me from total humiliation was that nobody in the room knew us. We eloped, had a civil ceremony, and the judge's elderly mother was our only witness.

Of course, I had to face my family and friends once I got home. Everyone begged to see my gorgeous wedding band, the one I had been bragging about since my fiancé proposed. I made up one excuse after another for not wearing it yet—my fingers were swollen, I misplaced it, etc.

This has now gone on for five years. The truth is simple but painful. My husband says he can't afford the ring I deserve. According to him, a quality diamond band is supposed to cost the equivalent of two months' salary, at least that's what he saw in a newspaper advertisement.

He now earns ten thousand a month, which means he could buy me a twenty-thousand-dollar ring! I made him aware of this fact. He squirmed out of the conversation by saying, "I expect a big raise in six months. If I get you a ring now it will be too cheap for you in half a year. I'm not going to let my wife walk around in a ring cheaper than she is!" In the meantime I should tell people that I'm allergic to diamonds.

He was so flustered, I let him off the hook once more. Meanwhile, he bought himself a new set of golf clubs.

I'm growing impatient and seeds of suspicion are starting to sprout. I may be forced to take matters into my own hands, so to speak. But a girl's gotta do what a girl's gotta do. I figure that's why God made credit cards.

I Tried to Be a Hooker But There Were No Takers

I was working as a waitress when I got laid off. It couldn't have happened at a worse time because I was in debt up to my eyebrows. I had just gotten back on my feet after breaking my leg in two places.

After I got over the shock of being fired, I had to face my money worries. I had no job, no family, and no rich friends. What I did have was a great figure. Which is crazy because I don't diet and hate exercise. I guess I'm just lucky.

I decided the best way to make a buck was to sell my best asset—my body. At first, just thinking about it made me blush. I couldn't imagine being in bed with a total stranger. On the other hand, I couldn't imagine starving to death.

I chose a singles bar across town. That way if someone was interested in me, it would seem natural to talk about a "price" for my company. When I got to the bar, I sat down and ordered a wine cooler. It was early, only 10 P.M., but the place was already crowded.

No doubt about it, guys were looking me over. But for some reason, nobody was making a move. I kept ordering drinks and hoping I wouldn't fall off the stool.

Just when I was ready to pack it in for the night, a good-looking "silver fox" kind of guy came over and started chatting me up. He was friendly and seemed interested. When he asked me out for coffee, I nervously told him men I go with pay for "dates." He just shrugged his shoulders and said politely, "No thanks. That's not what I'm looking for." Then he left.

I stayed for another half an hour and then went home—broke and alone. The next day I applied for and got another waitress job.

Later in the day I was sipping some coffee and nursing my wounded ego when I opened the newspaper. There was a story and photo of the man who had talked to me at the bar. He was being honored as salesman of the year by the real estate industry. The article pointed out he was a millionaire. He was also single. In the story he said, "I want to get married and have a family. I'm still looking for the right lady."

I didn't know whether to laugh or cry. In my pinheaded attempt to make an extra buck, I'd blown the chance to date a millionaire—and maybe become his wife. He was a nice guy, too.

I Forgot to Wear Underwear
on a Glass-Bottom Boat

Have you ever been intoxicated by a place? When I found myself in the Caribbean this past winter, I was drunk on the salt air and tropical breezes. You wouldn't have thought of me as the sort of person this would happen to. I'm a bookkeeper for a small Midwest manufacturing firm. I'm not fussy about my appearance. I usually wear tailored clothes and a simple hairstyle.

But that all went out the window practically from the first moment I stepped off the plane. The warm, sultry climate, the handsome people, the luscious food, and even the fabulous music made my head spin. It wasn't long before I lost sight of my girlfriend and was in a resort boutique buying clothes that made me feel like I'd "gone native."

Other people must have felt the same way because some of the women who'd been so covered up on the airplane were now topless on the beach! I don't have what it takes to be that bold but I just had to do something to express my newfound freedom. So on the morning of a harbor cruise, I put on a new black gauzy sundress, some bright beads—and nothing else. Without undergarments I felt sensuous and a little bit naughty. Demi Moore had nothing on me!

But my mood of joy turned to one of horror as the small vessel pulled away from shore. It was a glass-bottom boat! Not only that, half the people aboard were in scuba-diving equipment and when the boat anchored they began diving below. One man even looked up and waved at me.

For the next hour, I was consumed with trying to protect my modesty in every way you can imagine. I was so busy clutching my skirts around me in the brisk sea breeze, I didn't even bother looking at the beautiful ocean beneath me. It was the longest sixty minutes of my life.

On my next vacation I'm going skiing.

I Hate Me Because I'm Beautiful

It's left me alone and lonely, surrounded by an invisible barrier. My crime? I'm a natural-born beauty.

From day one, I was gorgeous. People begged my parents for my baby pictures. They even clamored to see my father's home movies of me toddling around in the backyard, my luscious auburn curls lit up by the sun.

I never went through that adolescent awkward age. I blossomed into a tall, slim, graceful knockout with eye-popping measurements, if I do say so myself.

As I grew into young womanhood, men stopped me on the street to offer me "modeling contracts" and phoned all hours of the day and night. By the age of fourteen, I needed a telephone answering service to screen my calls.

During my years in high school, I was the automatic prom queen. No one else was ever nominated. Everybody said, why bother?

You'd think every morning I'd want to kiss the mirror. Don't bet on it.

Beauty is hell. First of all, nobody trusts me. My plainer sisters don't want to be friends—and I really can't blame them. Next to me, they look like something from the barnyard. And men believe every cliché about a beautiful woman, assuming I'm arrogant, conceited, superficial, with cornflakes for brains.

As for my future, I'm truly terrified. I'm far too stunning to end up a nobody, which is what I want to be. My parents hound me to try modeling in New York or break into the movies. They say the money is too good to dismiss and that's what a girl like me is supposed to do.

I'm a junior in college now, majoring in physical geography. I'd eventually like to get into mapmaking and work for some scientific agency. But, everybody scoffs at my goal, saying I'd be too distracting in any office.

Sometimes in my dreams I'm homely but happy, surrounded by friends who love me just the way I am. Then I awaken to the stark reality of being beautiful and it hurts.

My biggest fear: I'll end up as somebody's Trophy Wife.

I Have Shopping Amnesia—
I Can't Remember a Thing I Buy

Wonderful clothes suddenly appear in my closet—but I can't remember purchasing them. I have sophisticated city outfits, dozens of jeans and tops, party dresses, and sexy lingerie. I have a wardrobe that would make a Hollywood starlet jealous. Yet when a friend asks when I bought that suit or where I ordered those shoes, I draw a blank.

Most every morning, when I get dressed for work, I find something new—price tags and all—hanging in my closet. Then I rack my brains trying to figure out how the darn thing got there.

The first time it happened I thought my husband had bought me a new dress as a gift. When I went to thank him, he looked at me funny and said, "It's not from me. Maybe your mom wanted to surprise you." But my mother had been gone all week. I asked my friends, even the pizza delivery guy. They all denied it.

When the credit card bill arrived, it all came out in the wash, so to speak. I had bought and signed for the new dress—a whopping $250, far more than my husband likes me to spend on myself. I was so shocked you could've knocked me over with a feather. I had to admit, though, it was a sensational outfit and did wonders for my figure. The inflated price tag didn't seem so awful when I looked in the mirror. I just told myself: "You're worth it."

From that day on, my wardrobe began filling up with more and more beautiful things. Naturally, my husband began to notice. He demanded that I put an end to my "endless shopping spree." But if a lady can't remember what she's doing, how can she stop?

At least I'm the best-dressed amnesiac in town.

I'm So Sensitive
I Hear Potatoes Scream When They're
Deep-Fried

Years ago when I began growing vegetables in a small plot of land next door to my house, gardening was my hobby. It was fun to see things grow and enjoy the fruits of my labor at the dinner table. Today, I could no more sit down to a meal of my own vegetables than I could to a meal of my own kids. Once I got to know vegetables, they were very much living, breathing creatures similar in many ways to my beloved offspring. They were no more a "hobby" than my family was.

My attitude changed slowly. I'd be working happily in my garden and I'd suddenly notice an especially adorable carrot or enchanting zucchini. I'd reach over to give it a pat and a bit of praise. Curiously, it seemed to respond to the compliment, maturing into the most beautiful fruit in the garden. In this way, I began feeling bonded to my plants. When their leaves were droopy or bothered by pests, I'd feel blue. When they looked perky, my spirits would soar.

But the event that changed my attitude forever was the day I fried my potatoes. They were the sweetest new potatoes I ever grew and I planned to serve them for dinner. I let the oil get bubbling hot, and then I tossed them in the pan. It was horrific! I heard those little potatoes scream in agony as they were fried alive. Naturally, I couldn't eat a bite and it was excruciating to watch my family gobble them down.

From that point on, I decided to allow my vegetables to live out their natural lifespan. I plant and tend my garden as usual. However, instead of picking the fruit, I let it die on the vine. My plants have a healthy and wonderful life—and a quiet, peaceful passing. I grieve silently, taking solace in the fact that I did my very best for them.

Because my family insists on eating vegetables, I buy them at the supermarket. I try not to think about where they come from but sometimes I wonder, "Whose little squash are you?"

A Ventriloquist's Dummy
Talked Me into Marriage

His name is "Benjamin Byrd" and I love him more than words can say. Because of my wonderful woodenhead, I'm now the mother of three healthy children and the wife of a hardworking provider.

It all started the day I met Ben's shy, soft-spoken human pal "Cliff." We worked together in different departments of a huge corporation. I first noticed him in the hallway: tall and good-looking, with a boyish modesty. I tried my girlish best to snare him into talking, but had no luck until we rode the elevator by ourselves one lunch hour.

Cliff sputtered and stammered, but was finally able to ask for a date. I was elated. Unfortunately, the evening became a disaster when Cliff could barely get a word out and spilled his soda on my new dress.

I wrote off the dress and the relationship until Cliff nervously invited me to play Frisbee with him and a friend in the park. I decided to give him one more chance and an hour later met him sitting on a park bench. There was a patent-leather suitcase beside him.

"Looks like your friend's late," I noted.

"No. He's right here," Cliff stammered. Then he eagerly

opened the expensive suitcase and lifted out a wooden dummy with wavy hair, a bulbous nose, and a goofy expression on his face.

The dummy's mouth opened. "Hi, doll! Benjamin Byrd here. What's a pretty thing like you doing with old stone face? He this week's charity case?"

I chuckled. "Don't say that. Cliff's a very sweet fellow."

"He's sweet, all right," Ben cackled, "sweet as a freakin' lemon."

I laughed again. Amazingly, I then proceeded to enjoy an hour's conversation with Ben, whom I found to be witty, charming, and quite wonderful. I was impressed that Cliff's lips didn't move the entire time. He was very talented.

Over the ensuing weeks and months, Ben and I talked endlessly nearly every day. Through him, I came to know Cliff very well. This magic time climaxed when Ben asked me to marry Cliff. I'll never forget Cliff down on one knee with Ben perched on the other.

We were wed in a civil ceremony, with Ben, of course, the best man in a tiny tuxedo I sewed for the occasion.

We've been married eight years now, with three wonderful kids. (He may not be much of a talker, but there are some great things Cliff can do on his own!) Sometimes, when we really want to get romantic, Cliff, Ben, and I snuggle under a blanket in front of a roaring fire—not too close, of course! Cliff and I let Benjamin do all the talking while we kiss and cuddle.

I Padded My Bra with Dollars—
and Bought Something Nice When I Filled Out
a 38D

To be honest, I've always been known for my personality, not my looks. I'm a positive thinker and naturally upbeat, so I have a lot of friends. The one regret about myself, however, is that I'm flat-chested. I don't really care all that much. But sometimes when I'm out with my husband, he stares at women with large breasts. After that, I feel bad for a while until I give myself a pep talk.

I decided to see what it feels like to be bigger on top, so I bought a bra in size 38D. Of course I had to stuff it with something to make it look real. I got this brainstorm. Instead of tissue paper, I'd put in dollar bills to fill out the bra. Then I'd wear a tight sweater to show off my new curves. And after that—to make myself feel better—I'd splurge with the money I'd used in my bra.

The "experiment" worked great. I went to the mall and strolled around. Men were really giving me the eye. I was excited and thrilled, finally learning what it's like to have "big boobs."

When I got home, I took off the bra stuffed with money and put my undershirt back on. I had a good $200 to spend for a gift on myself.

Chapter 5

Men

"Excuse Me, Sir,
Your Penis Is Showing"

I'll never forget the first words spoken to me by the woman who later became my wife. I've even toyed with the notion of having the sentence etched on my headstone to pay tribute to the memorable way it brought us together. But I'd rather keep it our little secret. I guess in Hollywood they would call the way "Gretta" and I met "cute."

Let me set the stage. I was a harried computer software salesman. Usually up before dawn, I dressed in the dark. People in the office said it looked like it. But in the software business, appearance isn't paramount. I was the top salesman in the corporation the day I hustled into the airport with just minutes to spare.

My mind was a blur of sales points and statistics as I hurried aboard with my briefcase, laptop, and raincoat. It wasn't until a few minutes later I realized just how lucky I was to be carrying that much crap.

Collapsing in my seat, I flipped open my laptop and began working so intensely I didn't even feel the jet start to taxi. It wasn't until I noticed a figure hovering over me that I snapped out of my trance. I turned to see the most beautiful slim, blond flight attendant in airline history. Her name tag said "Gretta."

Calmly, she bent over and whispered into my ear the fateful words that soon made the two of us one.

Groping with a free hand, I discovered she was right. I'd been in such a hurry that morning, I'd decided to skip the underwear stage. But forgetting to zip up hadn't been part of the plan. My face turning eight shades of red, I covered my lap with a vomit bag. Then I quietly shut my "barn door."

In a soft Scandinavian accent, Gretta murmured, "I speak frankly. It is my way."

Before we landed, I had regained sufficient composure to ask Gretta out for a thank-you dinner. I was amazed when she agreed. She joked that she felt she knew me very well already.

Wedding bells rang shortly thereafter. I now have a loving wife who makes sure I'm zipped up before leaving each morning. She says she doesn't want me impressing other women the way I did her.

I Could Have Been a Rock Star
If I Didn't Need to Be in Bed by Nine

I'm not going to be modest. I sling a mean guitar.

When I was still in my teens, one of the all-time "guitar gods" proclaimed me "The Next Big Thing." I had sneaked into the arena to watch this rock legend's afternoon rehearsal. I know this is bold, but I plugged into a spare amp and began trading licks with my idol. Two burly roadies were about to toss me out on my butt when The Legend stopped them dead in their tracks. "Back off, boys. Let him play," he muttered through a haze of cigarette smoke.

The stunned roadies retreated and I jammed with my hero for over an hour. By the time we were done, even the crew was cheering my riffs.

The Legend pulled me aside, "Kid, you've *got it*. Someday I'm going to be out in the audience and thousands of people will be going crazy listening to you!" When he asked me to jam onstage with him that night at the end of the show I almost passed out.

That's when my nightmare began. I'm a morning person. The best part of my day takes place before 8 A.M. It's all downhill from there until I can barely drag myself to bed by nine at night. I've been to doctors and sleep-disorder clinics by the score, but there's nothing they can do. My internal clock is set extra early and can't be changed.

By the time The Legend called me onstage at midnight, I was already three hours past my bedtime. I played the worst I ever have in my life. I stumbled around, wishing I was under the covers in my pajamas, blissfully asleep. The Legend never spoke to me again and a reviewer said I looked like I was on drugs.

Ten years have gone by now and I've given up hope of ever making it big. I've gotten a bad reputation in the rock community. One promoter said he'd give me a call if he ever started booking breakfast concerts. About the only kind of gig I'm called for is backing up a children's singer, but even I get tired of being pelted with chewed candy. And how many times can you play Barney's theme?

I've resigned myself to being the world's greatest guitarist— before noon!

Still Trick-or-Treating at Age Forty-Five

I have a sweet tooth the size of Alaska. That's why when Halloween rolls around I break out the old shopping bags and go begging.

Some people may say I suffer from a case of arrested development, but where on the law books is there a statute of limitations on trick-or-treating? I should know—I'm a lawyer.

At forty-five, it's not easy to look like a kid. I'm five-ten and two-hundred-plus pounds. In addition, I have the beginnings of a bald spot on the top of my head and a Richard Nixon five-o'clock shadow that's impossible to disguise.

But I'm nothing if not ingenious. Last year I taped wrapping paper and ribbon around some cardboard boxes and went as a stack of Christmas presents. All you could see of me was my baby blues through the eye holes. The optical illusion created by my arrangement of presents made it impossible to figure out my true height. I netted thirty pounds of candy, after tossing out the fruit and other junk like that.

One advantage of trick-or-treating at my age is that I have a longer stride and can cover more ground than the typical nine-year-old. Plus, I keep an up-to-date computer file on the best and worst neighborhoods for candy. It's based on a somewhat complex program that considers the number of lit and unlit porch lights, size of pumpkins, types of treats, etc. Each year, I eliminate homes that have been declining in two or more categories and carry the printout with me.

It really helps. For instance, there's a rich guy a few blocks away who always has full-size Hershey bars. The printout alerts me that the maid and butler alternate at the door, so I'm sometimes able to hit the house twice without anyone being the wiser.

As far as getting caught, the closest I ever came was three years ago at my parents' house. My mother seemed to recognize my voice when I yelled, "Trick or Treat!" But she's elderly, so I just grabbed and ran before she could put it all together. Boy, were my underarms wet.

But the best part of Halloween for me is the rest of the year. I can't tell you how satisfying it is to offer a client candy from the Wedgwood jar on my desk, then pop some into my own mouth. And only I know my Halloween secret.

My Wife's Makeup Got Me a Big Promotion

"Geez, you look beat, guy! You must have been burning the midnight oil on the new account," declared my twirpy little colleague as he strode jauntily by my desk.

My blood boiled. This wasn't the first time the punk had put me down in front of the entire office. I work in office supply sales, a dog-eat-dog business, and jerks like him are part of the atmosphere.

He was newly hired, a twenty-nine-year-old combination package of MBA and PhD—the whiz kid who was going to take us places, put the sales team on the map. While he looked fresh and snappy in his phony Armani suits, I was beginning to look permanently rumpled.

But getting older is a handicap in the office supply grind. If you aren't vice president by fifty, you're out the door. I was nervous. Fifty wasn't far off anymore. I needed my job—and my salary.

I was musing about the situation in bed one morning when I happened to glance at my wife doing her makeup. Why, I asked myself, shouldn't I take advantage of the enormous advances in cosmetic science? Hey, a little of this, a little of that could make all the difference in the world! Obviously, it works for a woman—why not for a man?

When my wife left for work, I sneaked over to her cosmetics drawer. There was goop for just about every need a face might have. I picked up a cover-up cream and dabbed a little under my eyes, smoothed on some bronze stuff and brushed my cheeks with a kind of powder.

Then I stood back and studied my face in the mirror. Not bad. It's not so much that I looked younger, just better. Unlike my former pallid self, I seemed like a man who was going places—such as a new corner office.

From that day on, I began sneaking my wife's cosmetics daily. I became pretty expert at doing my face, sometimes slipping into the men's room for a quick touch-up.

About a month later, I was promoted to V.P. Just before I left that day, I walked by the whiz kid's desk. "I want you thinking file cabinets over the weekend," I ordered. He didn't even try to smile.

The Burglar Was Nude

This was the Manhattan crime nightmare I'd dreaded. It was 3 A.M., a burglar was in our hotel room, and he was naked as a jaybird.

I'm a scrapper when it comes to the dry ice industry. But I haven't done much fighting on the physical front in twenty-five years. This is why I amazed myself by falling quickly into a kung fu crouch as I faced my attacker—all the more amazing since I don't know kung fu. None of this fazed the naked guy, who continued to bore holes in my skull as he mimicked my every move.

The last few days flashed before my eyes. My wife and I were in New York for the first time since we'd married two decades before. A lot had changed since then, chiefly three kids and less hair. But some transformations had been for the better. Money, for instance. On our honeymoon, we'd had no choice but to stay with friends and live on street-vendor hot dogs. Thanks to an increasing share of the dry ice pie, this time we relaxed in a posh Midtown hotel and dined at the finest restaurants.

After three days of sightseeing, I was ready to collapse, which I did until nature called around 3 A.M. I quietly slipped from my wife's arms and staggered sleepily towards the bathroom.

That's when I encountered the burglar and snapped into my martial arts fighting position. "You son of a b——. Get the hell out or you're finished," I hollered, my voice sounding like a wild animal ready for battle.

Of course, that awakened my wife. She screamed.

I inched to the left and the creep did the same. I stepped forward. And he did. *He was mocking me!* I hunkered down and charged.

Just then, my wife flicked on a light and I saw the brute in all his glory for the first time—ME. I was staring into a speckled mirror that covered one entire side of the bedroom. I was naked and had the face of a madman.

"Who is it, darling? Are we being attacked?" my wife shrieked, pulling the covers up to her neck.

"Uh . . . no . . . I'm just going to the bathroom. . . ." Then I broke down and told her the whole sad story, trying to portray myself in the best light—as a rough-and-ready damsel protector. I have to admit it felt good that I still was in shape enough to scare me.

Three-Day Ordeal:
I Glued Myself to My Easy Chair

I fought on the beaches of Iwo Jima, but I have never so feared for my life as when I glued myself to my recliner and battled for days to set myself free.

Day 1: At 0800 hours Friday morning my better half drove off to visit her sister for the weekend. I was on my own in the farmhouse to do just as I wanted. Play sports loud on the radio. Maybe even add a little whiskey to my beer.

1200 hours: I was still in my underwear, as is par for the course on such occasions. Exhausted from a failed attempt to glue the mast onto my latest ship-in-a-bottle, I retreated to my recliner.

An hour later I awoke, my mouth dry as bone. But when I attempted to rise, it was like a vise held my rear. I tried and failed again and again to get up. All at once I knew why. I had napped for an hour on a big tube of that super-grip glue. The chair, my boxer shorts, and my keister were stuck together like iron.

The escape effort had me even more parched. My eyes landed on the only fluid within reach: a half-quart of Johnny Walker Red on the end table. I sipped from it slowly, knowing it might be my only nourishment for days.

Day 2: I awoke disoriented in the dead of night. As I rolled about, the recliner tipped with a sickening crash and I was flat on the floor. The chair and I were still cheek to cheek.

Somehow, I drifted off again, only to be aroused by the dawn. I coolly analyzed my predicament. My only chance was to reach the phone on the other side of the living room. I clawed the carpet with my fingernails, barely inching along. By early evening the quart was empty and no longer of use.

Day 3: Sunday I resumed my arduous journey, a day full of fevered images of paramedics hovering over my dehydrated body.

Monday morning, 0900: I clawed forward with a jerk. Horrible pain ripped my rear. But I was free! I looked back to see portions of my boxer shorts and my bottom still stuck to the recliner.

An hour later I had consumed four bologna-and-egg sandwiches and a half gallon of milk. By the time I heard the little lady's tires crunching over the gravel, I had repaired my chair and policed the room. To this day, my wife has no idea where my red-and-blue polka dot boxer shorts disappeared!

I'm an Unemployed Male Bra Fitter

In fact, I've never had a job in my chosen career. Talk about discrimination—you should see the dirty looks I get just *asking* for a job application.

You might think it's a laugh—a husky guy with a Paul Bunyan beard in this line of work. That's why I haven't told anyone except my wife. But I'm a laid-off timber worker with a family and a mortgage to pay and I'm nothing if not a survivor.

I got the idea for this bra-fitting thing after watching my wife struggle with a new one a few months back. It didn't fit right. That's when I learned how awful some bra fitters can be, costing women millions a year in nonreturnable merchandise.

A light bulb went off in my head. Why didn't I give bra-fitting a shot? After all, I've always been good with my hands. The pay is good and you're not behind a desk. The perfect gig for a self-starter like me.

My wife was skeptical at first, but became quietly accepting as she noted how quickly I caught on. I owe everything to that wonderful lady. She even taught me the basic bra-fitter spiel: "Make sure you're all in the cup. Now bend over and shake!"

You'd think the industry would've jumped all over somebody as promotable as me—a self-taught male bra fitter. The publicity possibilities are enormous. I can just see me making the talk-show circuits. You know, I could do a live fitting on Cindy Crawford or some other supermodel. Or if the producers were looking for laughs, I could fit Roseanne or Jay Leno in drag.

As things snowballed, my own line of bras would be a natural. On the back by the clasp there'd be a tag: a drawing of me and my beard. Take a look at the mallard logo on those "Duck Head" pants and you'll get what I'm aiming at. The college girls would love it. Hey, I've got a whole portfolio of ideas.

Instead, I'm treated like some sort of pariah. Phone messages aren't returned, letters aren't answered. I've slammed head-on into the "Underwire Ceiling." Maybe that's what I get for trying to be a pioneer. I find solace in the belief that ten years from now, if even one male breaks into the business, it'll be thanks to my efforts.

I'm probably the only guy I know who goes to a topless bar and imagines how good the dancer would look in a nice strapless. I can't look at a woman without instantly sizing her up. 34D, 36C . . . I know I'm right, but how can you ask?

One day it's going to "happen" for me. Until then, I hone my skills and wait. Try that on for size, America!

In the Doghouse and He Loves It

Friends think I'm the kindest pet owner in the world. That's because of the elaborate doghouse I built for Buck, my three-year-old black Lab. Here are just some of the features: built-in space heater, overhead lights, running water and electric outlets for a hot plate, a portable TV, a computer, etc. It's big enough to sleep two comfortably. And it often does—Buck and me.

Yes, many a night I've fallen asleep to the sound of Buck's snores after being tossed out by my wife, Baby.

I got the idea after staging a strategic withdrawal one night from the house sans wallet, cash, and car keys. Yeah, the incoming crockery was pretty heavy. Sleeping on the deck held no appeal; it was raining. The only dry alternative was shacking up with Buck—he even had a blanket. His old doghouse was a tight squeeze. But Buck and I kept each other warm and he only got up once to bark at a raccoon.

That weekend I set to work. I own a construction firm and I've never lost my manual skills. First I laid a concrete foundation and on subsequent weekends I erected a sturdy log home with a shake roof and all utility connections. Friends ribbed me mercilessly and I took their jibes. I didn't want to reveal my hidden agenda.

After five weeks, Buck's new abode was ready. He took to it

immediately. Within ten minutes he was relaxing on one of two comfy cedar shavings mattresses.

That Sunday, after a twelve-hour football-watching marathon that drove Baby a little gaga, I joined Buck for the first time. It wasn't the last.

The problem is, I think Buck has started to sour on the new arrangement. When I woke up the other morning he was gone. Guessing that he was out after his enemy raccoon, I picked a few flowers from the garden and went upstairs to mend things with my wife. But when I entered the bedroom, there was Buck sleeping beside Baby—on my side of the bed. Jilted by my own dog!

Lazy Slacker:
Don't Tell My Friends I'm an Investment Banker

Because my disguise is perfect—greasy hair, wispy goatee, torn blue jeans, tattoos, and T-shirt—I look just like any other over-educated, underpaid Generation X-er. The only difference is that the goatee is glued on, the tattoos wash off, and I have a roll of hundreds in my pocket big enough to choke a horse.

I've never had much luck with girls or even pals. But when it reached the point I was spending Saturday nights in my apartment sailing paper airplanes made out of hundred-dollar bills, I knew I had to act.

I approached loneliness like they taught me in B-school: with a business plan. The problem: no social life. The solution: the Slacker—a person of my generation who does nothing but drink coffee and whine, but has plenty of company. After a trip to a costume shop I had perfected the look.

Now it was time to act. I found the nearest Starbucks, took a deep breath, and shuffled in. I felt obvious, like I was wearing an invisible power tie over my T-shirt. But no one batted an eye. Within fifteen minutes I was talking to people and even won a contest on who could blow the most creative smoke ring. Later, a bunch of us went on a walk, including a beautiful babe named Mary. We took turns writing graffiti with canned cheese spray, then came back and argued how long it would take the dog poop on one guy's shoes to dry. That evening I read from the back of a Count Chocula box at a Poetry Slam. I spent the night on a new friend's couch—with Mary.

To keep up appearances, I started working the weekend graveyard shift at 7-Eleven. Mary thinks it's cool because she can come in anytime for a free Slurpee. I know she's serious because she wants me to move in with her on the couch. How can I tell her I have a fifteen-hundred-dollar-a-month apartment with a wine collection that would pop your eyes out?

I don't have much time to decide because pretty soon Mary and I are going to have one more little latte to order—she's pregnant!

Chapter 6

Leisure

Liberace Is My Guardian Angel

This little lady never made the acquaintance of the great pianist when he was alive, but we've become tight since he died.

Whether I've discovered a new word at Scrabble or a strange hair in my salad, the master showman is with me through good times and bad. I've felt his warm hand on my shoulder, smelled his clove-scented breath on my neck, and otherwise held the hem of his glittering cape down the rough roadways of life.

Our relationship began when I bought a beautiful candelabra at the flea market for three dollars and sixty cents. Could it have belonged to Liberace himself? We can only speculate. A friend later told me that it was actually one of those Jewish candleholders, but she's Catholic, so what does she know?

An amazing thing happened when I came home. As I unwrapped the candelabra, a warm sensation engulfed me, similar to a hot flash. I gazed up to view the ethereal presence of Liberace himself, resplendent in ermine. Since then, Liberace's gauzy, angelic form has helped me in more ways than I can count. Once at the supermarket I was about to purchase a box of detergent when he moved my hand to the shelf below. Another national brand was on sale there. With that one gesture, Liberace saved me seventy-five cents.

The other day my special angel saved my life and the lives

of a good dozen other people when I almost ran over the curb on a crowded street. Liberace seized the steering wheel in his bejeweled hands and swerved as I awoke from an unscheduled nap. Luckily, I only grazed a parked BMW, so nothing terrible happened.

To make my guardian angel feel more comfy when he's here, I've had my husband Rick build Roman columns on either side of the garage door. He's also mirroring the whole front hallway and painting the patio furniture pink.

Rick doesn't know why, but Lee and I do!

I Built an Ant Farm Inside My Storm Window

Ants are an important part of the natural world. They're industrious, work well together, and live in intricate yet orderly communities. We can learn a lot from them. In fact, that's what I tell my students in the science class I teach at the local community college.

In order to give my neighborhood ants a warm place to stay each winter, I create an ant farm between the storm window and the regular one in my living room. All it takes is twenty pounds of sand and half a bucket of ants. They do the rest of the work. Within hours, they're digging tunnels that spread like the roots of a great tree.

Maintenance is low—just a few fly parts once in a while. Every morning, it's a pleasure to pull back the drapes and see what new wonders they've wrought. And who needs TV sit-coms when you have hundreds of live entertainers in the form of your very own ant colony?

During a cold snap I warm the ants with a hair dryer run along the windowpane. The best part of my hobby is spring-time, when I release that season's colony back to the wild. Watching them disappear one by one into their natural habitat fills me with quiet joy. It's hard to wait until the first frost of fall, when I can fill my front window up with sand and start all over again.

M.D.: My Very Private Mucus Collection

You are undoubtedly familiar with the various secretions that issue from our bodies. I like to say: if you're not leaking, you're dead.

Of course, each of these substances has been the subject of countless medical studies. Tens of millions of dollars and as many man-hours have gone into their analysis. However, I contend that one of these materials has been sorely neglected: common nasal mucus. For some reason, the research community has given the back of their hand to snot.

I can't remember the last time a medical get-together or cock-tail party with my fellow physicians involved a serious discussion of nasal fluids.

Why is snot not taken seriously by the medical establishment? I have my theory. To most people, physicians alike, nasal matter, including "boogers," is "humorous." Moreover, the various hornlike honks, assorted bleats and rasps we make when blowing our noses strike the adolescent funny bone in us all.

In short, my friends, mucus is the bastard cousin in the extended family of human secretions. So great is the prejudice against snot research that I have kept my own work in the field strictly secret.

I'm an "ordinary" family doctor with a comfortable practice. However, I haven't let that stop me from initiating what I feel will be a major contribution to medical science. From wastebaskets in my office, I have collected thousands of used tissues containing the nasal mucus of my patients. Each tissue has been catalogued, bagged, and is being kept in a large cardboard box in my temperature-controlled wine cellar.

What these facial tissues will one day say to us I honestly haven't the slightest idea. Perhaps, just perhaps, we will discover that each of us has a "signature snot," as distinctive as a fingerprint. To aid identification, a police detective could blow the nose of a suspect in addition to taking his prints.

This is pure speculation. All I do know is, that upon my death, my will instructs that my entire collection be donated to researchers, for them to do with as they see fit.

Think-Tank Expert:
I Do My Best Thinking in Topless Bars

As a think-tank expert, I'm responsible for the analysis of some of the most important domestic policy issues of our day: welfare reform, farm price supports, immigration policy, that sort of thing. The position papers issued by our institute have influenced legislation affecting all Americans.

It's a heady feeling, but not always an easy job. There's a dirty little secret about people in my business: they can succumb to "thinking block" just as novelists can fall prey to "writer's block." I was personally struck by such a crisis a short while ago and I went for days without a thought in my head.

I needed an opinion—*any* opinion—on a woman's issue for a leading senator. He required it on his desk first thing the next morning and it was already 7 P.M. The office was deserted, and there was not a woman in sight from whom I could elicit an "insider's" viewpoint. Girlfriend-wise I'd been "in between trains" for months. Calling a 900-line was out of the question: I'd found during a previous emergency that such calls would be traced to my extension.

Suddenly, I was struck by the idea of visiting a topless bar. The dancers were, after all, women, and the place would show up on my company credit card as a "restaurant." Enthused, I raced out the door with a legal pad and a handful of pencils.

To make a long story short, the evening was a rousing success. Those sweaty, hard-working ladies were an absolute inspiration! After three hours of careful observation, I felt I'd learned everything there was to know about women, inside and out. My analysis was on the senator's desk before he walked in the door! I don't know whether he ever used it or not, but that's par for the course in this town.

Since then, whenever I'm facing a deadline and my mind is empty, I pay a visit to one of our many exotic dance bars. Sure, critics might be shocked to find that important American policy is being written by a balding guy with a G-string tied around his forehead like a bandanna. But, hey, it's results that count!

Mail Carrier:
I'm the Reason You Get *Playboy* a Week Late

Contrary to what you're thinking, it's *not* because of the ladies. I actually read the articles in my spare time. They've featured some of our top thinkers, such as Ken Kesey and other heads like that. I can still almost quote the Bob Dylan interview line by line, even though it was two or three decades ago. Man, what a bizarre mind.

On my crummy government pay check, I have to cut corners

wherever I can. There's no room in my budget for magazine subscriptions, so I "borrow" reading materials from my customers for a few days.

I'm really careful, though. I never eat or drink anything when I'm flipping through the pages. I've even perfected a way to open and close those sealed plastic bags so no one can tell the difference and get pissed.

I originally learned how to save a buck during my hippie days. I hardly had any money then, so I scrounged around for necessities or traded goods. Remember the old bumper sticker: "Ass, Grass, or Cash. Nobody rides for free"? That was my mantra.

When I got tired of hawking incense at on-ramps, I took a job at the post office. I've been here for twenty-five years, still wearing my ponytail, still listening to classic rock. I've had a great ride. I get to walk around all day outside, without a boss breathing down my neck. In the summer, I can wear shorts and work on my tan. Plus, the fringe benefits are outstanding. Like the magazines. Thanks to you dutiful, paying subscribers, I have plenty of great reading material to look through. For free.

In its own small way, I consider this a revolutionary act against the capitalist system. I estimate that over the past twenty-five years, I've saved as much as twenty-thousand dollars in subscriptions that would have otherwise fallen into the hands of the media monopolies.

Excuse me, while I relax with somebody's copy of *Time*.

My Wife Thinks I'm Having an Affair—
But I'm Really Going Bowling

I really do love my wife but she has this thing about being classy. I'm not sure what she saw in me—because I come from the wrong side of the tracks.

I've tried to do the best I can as a husband and provider. We live in a nice neighborhood, the kids are doing well in school, and my mate doesn't have to work. I have nothing to complain about—except that my wife doesn't like me doing things she considers "low class." For example, if I wear my undershirt to breakfast on Saturday morning, she says I look like a bum. She makes me shower and shave and put on the kind of dressing gown Cary Grant used to wear in those old movies of the 1930s. Anything to keep the peace!

Well, one of my passions in life is bowling. As you can imagine, my spouse just sniffs when I mention it. She tells me to find a better hobby and then leaves copies of snob magazines like *Town & Country* around, so I can read how croquet is back in style again!

Here's the topper: My wife has been hinting around that she'd like me to take a mistress—it's so *très* French! I'm just not built that way, but I'm so used to humoring her I decided to play along. Last month, I told her I was working late and instead went to the lanes. I bowled a few lines and drank a beer or two. But before coming home, I dabbed some woman's cologne and lipstick on my shirt and messed up my hair.

I tried to look distracted when I walked in the door, like I just spent the evening with "the other woman." As my wife gave me the once-over, a mysterious smile crept over her face. The next morning she was humming contentedly as she dabbed the lipstick stain off my shirt. That evening, she made my favorite dinner and fixed herself up for no particular reason.

Now when I have the urge to go bowling, I call my wife and tell her I'm "working late at the office." From the delighted sound of her voice, I know she thinks I'm going to visit my mistress. Go figure. Then I grab my gear and head for the lanes.

If only my bowling scores would improve.

Don't Tell My Wife—
But I Quit My Job Six Months Ago
Because I Make More Money as a Panhandler
on the Streets . . .

I was just like any other twenty-three-year-old guy. I had a wife and a new baby to support.

After high school, I got a sales job in a store that sells athletic shoes. My boss told me that if I worked hard and accepted responsibility, I'd be in line for a promotion. Basically, I worked my butt off. I hustled customers and did the usual grunt work necessary in the retail business. I also made a point to suck up to my boss to keep reminding him I was "manager material."

But after four years, I was still a "sales associate" and no closer to becoming a manager than I was the first day on the job. Every time I tried to talk to my boss about it, he just said, "Later, guy."

Business slowed down a lot after last Christmas, so my employer laid off some workers. Then he asked me to take a pay cut. I was told that if I wanted to stay on I'd have to accept minimum wage. I'd be making less than I did when I started the job!

When I left work that day, I was in a fog. Maybe that's the reason I lost my wallet. I had stuffed it in my jacket and when I needed it to buy a bus ticket it wasn't there. That meant I had no money to get home. I didn't even have any change in my pants pocket. So I did what others have done in that spot—I asked people to help me out.

After the first time, it wasn't so hard. In fact, the second guy who gave me money dropped a ten-dollar bill in my hand. By that time I had enough money to buy five bus tickets. I was so amazed by all the money I was getting for free, I didn't want to stop.

An hour later I was twenty dollars richer. In other words, I made almost five times more than had I worked for minimum wage during that time!

The next day I quit my job. Then I walked to the bus terminal, hung out, and picked up sixty-seven dollars in seven hours of panhandling. When I got home, I pretended that nothing had changed. My wife asked me how things had gone at work and I just said, "Fine."

The following morning I got dressed for work and left the apartment at the usual time. Then I headed for the airport where I picked up thirty-five dollars for a morning's work. I wanted the afternoon off—I felt I needed the break.

I couldn't believe how easy this was. Now that I've been panhandling half a year, I know I'm finished with the nine-to-five world. I'm making more money doing nothing than when I had a "real" job. I used to knock myself out for barely above minimum wage. Now I get plenty of fresh air and exercise while people drop money into my hands. I'm ten pounds thinner and my blood pressure is ten points lower.

But, I can't tell my wife. She always wanted to be married to a guy in management, so she wouldn't understand.

I Threw Up on a Twenty-Topping Pizza and None of My Fraternity Brothers Even Noticed

I'm a party animal. As far as I'm concerned, the four food groups are Bud, Miller, Pabst, and Old Milwaukee. But even I have to admit that things went a little too far on a recent Friday night. My frat brothers and I were having our usual T.G.I.F. kegger that would end sometime around Monday morning, when the last man standing fell face-first onto the floor. It was our way of letting off tension after a week of playing softball and chasing women, not necessarily in that order.

Anyway, I'd gotten tired of always waiting in line at the keg. So I decided to break into the old piggy bank and buy my own keg, which I hid under my bed. It was great. I would excuse myself from the action downstairs, race to my room like I had something to do, and then pour myself a tall, cold one. Towards the wee hours, it got so I was spending more time in my room than downstairs. I was like a kid with a new toy.

Finally, maybe around 3 A.M., I found myself alone on the front porch in my underwear when some guy dressed in a chicken suit delivered a massive, steaming, twenty-topping pizza. I was hungry, so I paid him for it. But when I sat down to scarf a few slices, my world came unglued. My stomach felt like a volcano had erupted and my brain took a quick trip to Mars.

When I came to, there was an additional topping on the pizza. I'd barfed all over it! But I have to say one thing: it was still steaming. Just then about a half dozen of my frat brothers burst out of the house screaming at me for hogging the pizza. I was too sick to say anything. I just sat there in the darkness watching them slurp it down.

But I got mine. When I went upstairs to call it a night, there was some guy asleep in my bed with his arms around my keg. He'd drained it dry.

I Listen to Country Music at the Opera

Have you ever heard a dozen hound dogs howling when they've got a raccoon up a tree? That's what opera sounds like to me, especially when all those fat people are carrying on at once. Yet I'm forced to go five or six times a year, because my husband's a devoted buff. Not to mention he's a prominent lawyer and to keep on top of the social whirl in this city attendance at the opera is a must.

Me, I have humbler roots. I grew up to the sound of grandpa playing the fiddle on the family farm. The social whirl revolved around shucking corn and picking cotton.

Opera singing really grates on me. The people are so pretentious and they yell like they're about to bust a gut. I've heard prettier sounds coming out of a hog caller. And those opera types don't kid around when it comes to blubber. The ladies look like they could stop an eighteen-wheeler with a single blow. The men remind me of overcooked hot dogs ready to explode from their skins. When the world-famous "Three Tenors"—Pavarotti, Placido Domingo, and some other lard ass—stand next to each other, I swear the stage sags.

So I attend the opera with my husband, but only on one condition—that I don't have to listen. When the house lights go down, I sneak a Walkman out of my evening gown. Discreetly putting on the earphones, I'm transported to a down-to-earth world where men wear cowboy boots and if women weigh over two hundred pounds they go on a *diet*!

While the posh crowd is listening to the baying of hounds, I'm serenaded by a tape of my favorite country stars. I listen to real men like Clint Black, instead of some balloon-bellied circus clown who can't even sing in English.

Sports Fan: I Found True Love in the Men's Room

Cupid is weird. You never know when that chubby fellow is going to draw back his bow and fire. An arrow pierces your heart. You look up and there's the love of your life with a big, wide grin that sets your body aflame.

I'm a believer in destiny. I think there's a special someone out there for everyone. You never know when your paths will cross. But, boy, when they do, you better seize the moment. You may never have such a good chance at romance again. Whether you're in Central Park or on the Golden Gate Bridge, you'd better "go for it" with every bit of passion in your soul. You might turn your life topsy-turvy, but at least you'll face the brave new world with love by your side.

For me, "it" happened during a lull in the third quarter of a college football game when I bolted into the men's room and took my place in line. Then Cupid fired his shot. I heard a woman's voice behind me, spun around and saw "Judy" for the very first time. Her hair was raven, her figure was perfect, and her jaw was set with fierce determination.

"Haven't you ever seen a woman before?" she challenged me.

"Not in here."

"Get used to it. The line for the ladies' room is a mile long. I'm not waiting there until my kidneys burst. I need to go to the bathroom."

Nearby, a few guys began to grumble. They didn't like the idea of a woman invading their space. But I admired her spunk. When I saw a fellow leave a stall, I hustled Judy inside, then turned around and guarded the door.

She came out with a lovely, relaxed smile on her face. This girl was a fighter and I wanted to be on her side.

"Want some coffee?" I asked.

"That's what got me in trouble in the first place," she joked.

We kept talking as we went outside and gabbed so much the game was over before we knew it.

Judy and I have now been dating for a year. She made me swear on a stack of Bibles to never reveal how we met, but I just had to share our little secret.

You might think I've become a staunch advocate of extra bathrooms for women. Not on your life. I don't want to deprive others of the same chance Judy and I had. Neither does Cupid, I think.

Chapter 7

Family

I Forgot My Father's
Dying Wish

It's haunted me for two long years since his passing. I've been through every kind of therapy you can imagine, from hypnosis to some of the nuttier things, and I still can't remember.

My ordeal began the moment Dad summoned me into his hospital room. Per his request, the rest of our clan remained in the hallway, behind the closed door. I knew what was up. Dad was going to make one last statement before dying, a message I was to relate to our grieving family outside.

With a heart thumping against my rib cage, I took Dad's cool hand in mine. Dad and I had a special relationship. He was a difficult man, but he'd always been my hero, a tall outdoorsman, strong as an oak. It had ripped me apart to see him shrivel up during his final months.

Not to disparage my brothers or my elderly mother, but Dad knew I'd carry out his last request if it killed me. He called me the dependable one. At family gatherings he'd always announce that when his time finally came, he'd have something of vital importance to say, and he'd tell only me. That time had come.

With one last great effort, Dad lifted his mouth to my ear, uttered two or three sentences, then collapsed. I was too overcome with emotion to hear much. But before I could ask him to repeat himself, he was gone.

After closing his eyes, I steeled myself to tell the others. I entered the hallway and was greeted by cries of "What did he say?" and "What did Dad tell you?"

The truth hit me like a punch to the stomach. "I . . . I . . . don't remember!" I stammered. The floor swirled and I swooned.

Since that fateful day, I've spent more money on experts than I care to add up. Still, I'm a complete and total nerve-wracked blank.

Only one thing gives me peace. I know that if I don't remember in this lifetime, Dad will remind me when I join him in Heaven. I can almost hear him gently chastising me, "How many times do I have to tell you? This time write it down!"

I Threw My Son's Little League Game

It isn't easy being a father when your kid is involved in sports. I've stared victory, defeat, and even death in the face during the course of my ten-year-old's career. That's right, death. Problem is, I blinked. To save my own skin, I caused "Mark's" team to lose the city championship.

My story starts three years ago, during Mark's rookie year in T-Ball. His team was playing a make-or-break game against some kids sponsored by a guy I'll call "Vic." Vic was an ultra-competitive businessman with a lot riding on the outcome: the reputation of "Vic's Ice Cream Bin" and the fact that his son "Luke" had the final at-bat.

Luke struck out in three swings. I let out a triumphant howl, which apparently made me Vic's eternal enemy.

In the seasons to follow, there were problems whenever our boys played each other. I pulled off and stomped on Vic's glasses once and he broke my toe when he tripped me. Another time I melted his ice cream cone with my lighter. I'm certain he passed gas every time he walked by.

Then came the day Vic arrived at the diamond packing heat. There was the unmistakable shape of a gun under his sport coat as he stood in line for popcorn. The message was clear: he planned to kill me if Luke lost again.

My life flashed before my eyes as Mark's team entered the final inning with a commanding 23–0 lead. It was time to act or die. As a teammate of Luke's was rounding third for what appeared would be an inside-the-infield home run, I leapt over the fence in pursuit. Wrapping my arms around him, I acted like I was upset Mark's team was going to lose its shutout.

The crowd went berserk. The ump charged me with interference and ordered the game forfeited to the opposition. You should have seen Vic's smug grin as he hopped about in a grotesque victory dance. It was only then I saw his "gun" was an ice cream scoop shoved in his back pocket. He'd bluffed me big and won.

I lie awake nights hoping I haven't hurt Mark's major league chances.

"May Your Mother Live to Be One Hundred": Secret Curse Comes True!

Mom wasn't what you'd call "maternal." Instead of baking cookies and wiping away the tears of her seven kids, she shot pool through the day at the tavern down the street. My long-suffering dad put up with it because he adored her—and because she was a pool hustler par excellence.

This was New York, circa 1933, when adults were so worried about money they didn't notice what us kids were doing. I went to Coney Island a lot with my pals. We had a ball. On one visit, my best friend dared me to see the fortune teller. With her wild hair and fierce expression, she looked like something out of a horror movie. But I didn't want to seem like a chicken so I walked into her small overheated studio.

She studied me for a minute, puffing on a smelly cigar, then offered to read my palm for a flat fee of a buck. I didn't have that kind of money on me. I figured I'd run when it was over. What was she going to do—call the cops on a kid?

In the next ten minutes I learned my future consisted of marriage, family, and money troubles. Plus, an occasional bout of constipation.

When the reading ended, the gypsy held out her hand. I tried to smile, hoping to earn a freebie with my freckle-faced charm. She saw instantly she was getting stiffed and thrust her arm in the air. I thought her fist was going to come down on my head. Instead she waved it and bellowed the fateful words: "May your mother live to be one hundred!"

"Thanks," I stammered.

"That's a curse, you cheapnik!"

I ran.

I forgot about the gypsy's secret curse until my frail, long-lost mom showed up on my doorstep at the age of seventy-eight, suitcase and pool cue in hand. That was twenty-two very long years ago.

Today, Mom still drinks scotch before noon, naps after lunch, then visits the neighborhood pool hall where she shows her winning form. One plus, though: she only yells at me when I forget to polish her cue.

Sometimes I think I hear the fortune teller laughing in my ear.

I Took Maternity Leave for
a Litter of Kittens

Okay, so I told my boss a little white lie: it wasn't my daughter who was going to give birth, it was my sleek Burmese cat. I simply couldn't let her go through the experience of motherhood alone.

Plus, it was my fault. Princess Baklava had come into "puberty" and I had a handsome, long-haired dreamboat selected as her first romantic partner. I often imagined the silken bundles of joy which would issue forth from such a blessed union.

Instead, I turned my back one day and Princess flew out the door, hell-bent for action of the most naughty kind. I was frantic with worry, imagining the most unfortunate scenarios. My precious Princess was looking for love on the "mean streets"— and any Tom, Dick, or Harry could end up her beau.

It wasn't until well after her bedtime that I found her meowing plaintively on the porch. Alas. I knew instinctively my worst fear had been realized: Princess Baklava was an innocent no more. In the space of a single moonlit encounter, my little kitten had become a cat. My heart broke as I reckoned with the consequences of her rash behavior. There would be offspring by some unknown cad. I imagined him lurking in a dark alley, just waiting to violate another innocent soul.

Soon enough Princess began to show symptoms of impending motherhood. Always a delicate eater, she now refused all but her favorite treats and showed no interest in kittenish games. Her slender frame filled out and her light step was replaced by a heavy waddle. Increasingly, she wanted only to nap.

I couldn't imagine leaving her alone to cope like some unwed Victorian waif, so I requested maternity leave. After all, why punish the babies because of a mistake of the mother?

We spent the night she gave birth in the hall closet together. By morning, the sound of six perfect babies mewing contentedly made me forget the untoward circumstances in which they came into the world.

Bored Housewife Makes More Money Than Hubby on Secret Job

"Hank" was a Neanderthal when I married him fourteen years ago and he hasn't changed. Not that he has fur on his back—he's a caring partner, a wonderful father, and a generous friend and neighbor. It's just that he doesn't want a working wife, especially while the kids are still in school.

I see his point, but the problem is I have too much energy to confine myself to the house. I only need about four hours' sleep a night and get restless if I have to sit longer than fifteen minutes.

By 7 A.M., even before my husband leaves for work, the house is spotless, the kids are ready for school, and I have fresh bread baking in the oven. By 8 A.M., the bills are paid, the dog is walked, the yardwork is finished—and an endless day lies ahead.

One boring afternoon, I got an idea. Maybe I could make a few bucks cleaning and organizing other women's houses while they were busy at work. I'd still be home in time to greet the kids and finish preparations for dinner, plus I'd have some extra money in my purse at the end of the day! Sure, Hank would be in the dark about it, but Neanderthals aren't supposed to strain their brains.

At first I spread flyers to attract business, then relied on word of mouth to expand. I now have more customers than even I can possibly handle, so I'm looking for a partner. I figure I'm bringing home about two hundred dollars more a month than Hank, which would hurt his feelings if he knew. And it's not pretty seeing a caveman cry.

Maybe someday I'll let Hank in on my secret, about the time he tells me why there's always a pinball machine in the background when he calls home late from "work."

I Destroyed My Sister's Marriage with Lasagna

Who says revenge is a dish best served cold? I've found that dishing it up piping hot with Parmesan cheese on the side works best of all.

This secret involves me and my older sister Pepper, a ravishing redhead. I'm a drab brunette in my twenties, so ordinary you couldn't pick me out of a police lineup.

Pepper has always been conceited about her good looks. Even as kids, she refused to use the same bathroom mirror as me. Said I spoiled the view.

Pepper demands perfection from her men, too. She once walked out on an absolute stud because he developed a chin pimple while they were chowing down at Pizza Hut.

Her quest for perfection ended eighteen months ago when she exchanged rings with a Tom Cruise lookalike at a church wedding that cost my parents a fortune.

My part in the great pageant was specifically limited to whipping up a platter of Patty's Perfect Deep-Dish Lasagna. All my life I've had only one talent: cooking. I had to do something on all those lonely evenings. And lasagna is my specialty. I developed my own recipe, using three kinds of cheese, homemade pasta, and a rich tomato sauce. Your cholesterol level shoots up ten points just by looking at it.

"Tom Cruise" sneaked a few bites at the reception, lifting his eyes heavenward as he ate. It was the most excited reaction I'd ever had from a man. This put thoughts in my head. I started dropping off a platter for him and Pepper every Friday at their apartment. In one month, he gained four pounds. This ended when Pepper met me at the front door and dumped the entire tray in the shrubs.

A week later, I received the shock of my life. "Tom Cruise" phoned to meet me for lunch in the parking lot where he worked. We had a magical picnic in the backseat of his car. He licked my lasagna plate clean, my smile growing bigger with every slurp.

Tom had a hidden hunger that only I could satisfy. We began to "do lunch" regularly in the parking lot. His car. My lasagna. Tom was ravenous.

One year and sixty-three pounds later, Pepper tossed her new husband out the door. Said he disgusted her.

Sure, he now looks more like John Goodman than Tom Cruise, but that's all right with me. We've been living together for six glorious months and are planning a trip to Italy, birthplace of his favorite dish.

I Ate Thanksgiving Dinner for Six

Okay, so their favorite daughter-in-law divorced me the day before Thanksgiving. Did that mean my family had to stand me up cold?

"Anita" and I were only married five months. So what that my dad paid for our Nashville honeymoon? Marriage doesn't come with a money-back guarantee, and if it did, I'd demand a refund myself. After all, I bought Anita an expensive umpire's uniform and she's probably bouncing with some guy on the inflatable chest protector as I write this.

It should come as no surprise that Anita and I met during a softball game. She was the ump and I was the star player for a lumber yard. I accidentally knocked her down sliding into first. She fell on top of me and it was love at first sight. (Incidentally, I was safe.)

Things went to hell before the ink was dry on our marriage certificate. Anita liked being a housewife more than an ump, whereas softball was my life. I played in three leagues and was never around. By the time the holidays came, she didn't want me home anyway.

Thanksgiving has always been a big thing with my family and we host it on a rotating basis. This year was my turn and I was determined to make it a roaring success, despite no Anita.

I blew most of my paycheck on turkey, trimmings, pumpkin pie, you name it. Everybody was supposed to show up by 4 P.M., after which we'd watch the football games while snacking. By 6 o'clock, no one had arrived and by 8 P.M., it was clear my family was making a statement. They weren't going to show.

I thought it was high time I made a statement myself. Tucking in my bib, I pulled myself up to the dinner table and went to work on the food.

Maybe anger gives you a great appetite, because it was like I hadn't eaten in a week. In short order, I gobbled down half the turkey, a mountain of mashed potatoes drenched in butter, and a bowl of green beans. I slaked my thirst with a quart of eggnog, then proceeded to demolish the salad without taking a break. As the football game blared, I ate half a dozen dinner rolls soaked in gravy, then devoured the rest of the turkey.

After an hour, I was feeling woozy, but I didn't let that stop me. I downed a jar of black olives like popcorn and finished off a box of Ritz crackers and a crock of cheese spread. Then I drank the rest of the gravy right out of the bowl. Dessert was the pumpkin pie and an entire canister of Cool Whip.

To this day, I have no idea when the game ended or who won. All I remember was calling Anita in a fog and gloating that Thanksgiving dinner was done and there wasn't a scrap left on the table. Who needed her?

I passed out on the couch and think I woke up around Christmas.

My Fiancé Doesn't Know It,
But I'm Going to Be a Virgin Forever

I haven't told him yet. I want it to be a surprise. Call me a naïve little country girl, but I think it'll strengthen our marriage.

When "Boyd" and I started dating, I explained I was old-fashioned and chastity was important to me. He simply said, "That's cool. I've always wanted to marry a virgin." He learned good values on the family farm, even though he didn't have much company other than his dog and sixteen thousand chickens.

Our romance blossomed into love and now we're making plans for our future. Boyd still treats me like a princess, even though he grinds his teeth a lot and gets headaches.

I noticed it wasn't the same with the girls who slept with their boyfriends. After a while, the guys stopped being nice, acted bored, and began roaming. Even after they married.

That's why I've decided to keep my virginity forever. It's the only way I can guarantee Boyd's lasting interest. This way, he'll probably stick around, treat me right, and be there for the chickens.

Chapter 8

Special Section:
Secret Opinions

Secret Opinions. We all have them. We just never tell a soul. So we've created a place where people can spout off—anonymously, of course.

Shower First to Enter Building

"I believe that all public buildings should have showers installed at the entrance. Then, if somebody smells bad, they'd be required to bathe before entering the premises. I got the idea when I was at the library one hot summer day and a jogger sat next to me. I didn't even have to glance at his sweatsuit to know he'd just finished a run. His aroma was not conducive to studying the great classics of literature! By the way, soap and towels could be provided by civic-minded organizations."

Let's Ban Mirrors

"Of all the pointless inventions humankind has come up with, nothing beats the mirror. People spend countless hours checking themselves out in front of mirrors—a monumental waste of time. If you're good-looking, mirrors make you vain and smug. If you look like a dog, you'll develop an inferiority complex the size of King Kong. If we ban mirrors, folks would have more time to spend with their families or doing something good for somebody."

Three-Minute Sex Is the Key to Success

"People whine about not having enough time, but I have found there are all sorts of ways you can save it. For example, I have sex in three minutes flat. By dispensing with the lengthy preliminaries, I free up valuable time to attend night classes, learn a new hobby, even do volunteer work. And there's no male chauvinism here. I'm all woman!

"Here's how I slash time at the supermarket: Upon entering the store, I search for a full cart that has been 'abandoned.' I push it quickly to another aisle, remove unwanted items, then wheel it into the checkout line. Bold? No! I'm simply exercising my salvage rights to unattended shopping carts left behind by harried shoppers. There are countless other ways to save time, if people would just think."

C-Span Is an Aphrodisiac

"Henry Kissinger once said that power is an aphrodisiac. This makes C-Span the most concentrated source of sexual stimulation I know.

"Where else can you leer at an endless parade of senators, representatives, and lobbyists exuding power from every male pore? Sure, most of the guys have hair weaves and half of them are barely breathing, but they can create 'pork' with a wave of their hand. And men with billions to blow make this little lady's motor run fast.

"When just the name Trent Lott makes you swoon, you'll know you're in the full grip of that erotic C-Span effect. Enjoy!"

Create Two Americas

"Let's end the war between the sexes once and for all. I propose creating two countries: the United States of American Men and the United States of American Women. Segregate the sexes so each gender can go its own way and do what it wants. Men can belch, pick their nose, not shave for a few days—and not offend any passing female. Likewise, women can spend all day on their hair and makeup, gab nonstop with their best friends, and no beleaguered male will be climbing the walls. If they desire sex, couples will need to go to a no-man's land between the two nations."

The World Will Run Out of Pop Songs by 2002

"Friend, it's already happening. Just listen to the radio: Doesn't every song sound like one you already heard before? Don't blame the songwriters. There are only just so many combinations of notes, strings on the guitar, keys on the piano—and we're coming to the end of the road. By my calculations, the industry will need to embark on an official recycling program just after the turn of the century. I advocate starting over with 'Down By the Old Mill Stream' and working our way up from there. The public can vote on tunes they don't want to hear again, like 'The Piña Colada Song.' "

Beauty Tip: To Tighten Skin, Add Pancake Batter and Bake

"Here's a helpful hint on how to beautify your skin while tempting your tastebuds. First, mix enough pancake batter to make half a dozen tasty flapjacks. Buckwheat or whole wheat, any kind of batter will do. However, I recommend against adding blueberries. They tend to run off the face, leaving almost indelible blue streaks that can be difficult to hide even with a heavy foundation.

"Next, lie flat on your back on a smooth surface. Position your head under a sunlamp, then ladle batter on face. You'll feel the baking batter close those pores almost immediately. Pull off pancake when dry and place on a plate. Add butter and syrup, then enjoy. Repeat procedure until your tummy is full and your face is glowing!"

We Must Build a Rock 'n Roll Mount Rushmore

"True rock 'n rollers are a dying breed. I say if you ain't got a bald spot or stretch marks, you ain't old enough to have been *there*, if you know what I mean. However, rock 'n roll will *never* die if we chisel the heads of Hendrix, Elvis, Dylan, etc., on the side of a mountain. Then future generations will have a permanent record of just what us rockers have wrought. Actually, there are so many rock legends, you might have to scatter the heads around, like those Tiki gods on Easter Island."

Require a Permit to Be Called an Adult

"A dog needs a permit. A garbage hauler needs a permit. A restaurant owner needs one to cook a pot of spaghetti. You even need a permit to clip another person's fingernails, for heaven's sake. I believe you should also have to win a permit in order to become an official 'adult.' This way, a nitwitted, immature forty-three-year-old would be prevented from driving a car, having legal sex, or drinking anything stronger than a Shirley Temple. On the other hand, a fourteen-year-old with a head on her shoulders could sign contracts, perform a marriage, even run for office.

"Based on a recent trip to a crowded shopping mall, I'd estimate that only about ten percent of the population would qualify as adult by such strict standards."

Let People Live in Disneyland

"There's enough homelessness in the world without leaving a bunch of perfectly decent buildings devoid of permanent residents. The whole theme park could be subdivided according to a person's background. For example, people of European heritage could live on the Matterhorn, hopeful but homeless students could study the future at Tomorrowland, and South

American–refugee types could enjoy the just-like-home humidity of the Pirates of the Caribbean. Think of Main Street as a tax-free enterprise zone where young entrepreneurs could get a start.

"In fairness to Disney, the homeless would still have to pay to go on the rides."

Replace Troublemaking Teens with Clean-Cut Actors

"It's like this: we've got more teenage punks than we'll ever need and not enough jobs for up-and-coming young actors. Both problems can be eliminated at once by shipping the bad apples to youth homes and replacing them with talented thespians. Just think—one day the neighborhood troublemaker is a graffiti-spraying, boom-box–playing foul mouth. The next day he's a trained actor, well-rehearsed in playing the role of the polite, well-groomed boy next door. While cleaning up the streets we'll be creating opportunities for the next generation of child actors."

Female Scientist: Big Penis = Low IQ

"This is an admittedly unscientific opinion, but from my personal experience and that of my colleagues, I can conclude the bigger the penis, the dumber the man. My theorem: well-hung men are more inclined to have 'brains between their legs' than their less well-endowed brethren. And no Nobel Prize has ever been awarded for work done by a man's 'little buddy.' Of course, my conclusions should be tested under strict conditions in a laboratory setting."

National Sex Holiday a Must

"This would be a great midsummer holiday to stop people from skipping work to have outdoor sex. I live near a public park and there's so much thrashing about in the bushes some afternoons you'd think we'd been invaded by hordes of giant horny rabbits. Except that these rabbits are human and they've abandoned their office cubicles for a romp under the sun. I advocate getting this fooling around all over at once with a nationwide day off for workers. This way, business phones would be answered again on summer afternoons and the word 'nooner' would be consigned to the round file of history."

To Find Love, Make War

"War is a time of heightened passion, when lovers cling to each other, never knowing when they'll see each other again. I should know. I met and married my wife just three days before I was shipped off to Europe during World War II. We've been married fifty-one years. I know this may sound nuts, but maybe we need another great war to solve the divorce problem in this country. Couples who meet under life-and-death conditions stick together."

Warning: Men Can Catch PMS from Women

"I'm convinced PMS is actually a highly contagious disorder. Every month, my wife's headaches, crying jags, extra pounds, and bad nerves are passed along to me. I guess it's some sort of sympathetic response—or that syndrome where the hostage starts to identify with his captor. The only difference between my PMS and hers is that I don't complain about men. I can handle most of the symptoms, except for the tears: I hate crying in front of my buddies."

To Decrease Deficit, Create XXX-Rated Stamps

"The Elvis Presley stamp sold like hotcakes, filling government coffers with cash. Now I have an even better idea—sex stamps with scantily clad men and women in all sorts of poses. Connoisseurs of this sort of filth would snap them up by the armload. Then they'd probably never use them, which would help balance the budget. Softer R-rated versions could be made for decent folk who just want to mail something."

To Increase Sex Pleasure, Suck a Lemon

"I know this sounds perverted, but one time I was sucking a lemon while fulfilling my wifely duty. Usually I eat an orange, but there wasn't one left in the fruit bowl on the nightstand. Somehow, the tart juice made me much more interested in what we were doing and I had the best sex I've ever had. It must be because your whole body gets puckered up or something, not just your mouth. Anyway, you might want to try it next time. The brand was Sunkist."

A Note to Our Readers

Tell the whole country your most intimate and personal secret.

Take advantage of our exclusive 100-percent-anonymity offer. Just write and tell us what you've never told anyone else. The story of your secret may wind up in print—without a soul knowing it's from you.

Mail to:

The Secrets Exchange
2852 Willamette #394
Eugene, OR 97405

Do You Behave Like Everyone Else?

From sea to shining sea, Americans are remarkably alike, incredibly different, and just plain strange. In this clever, fun and fascinating peek into the private lives of real Americans, columnist Bernice Kanner shares a delicious slice of American pie with humorous facts like:

- Of the half of us who have pets at home, 45.5% allow them in the room during sex.

- One out of every four ice cream orders is vanilla; only one in nine is for chocolate.

- Four out of ten of us admit we've been so mad we've hurled footwear at another person.

- Almost one quarter of us regularly check ourselves out in store windows and mirrors.

- 7 out of 100 Americans have flossed their teeth with their hair.

ARE YOU NORMAL?
Bernice Kanner

Bristling with the raw power of reality, this riveting book recounts true tales of life and death from the emergency rooms of America. Dr. Mark Brown asked over 15,000 fellow ER staffers to share their most unforgettable moments. Now, in their own voices, these real ER personnel bring us their most poignant, heartbreaking, laugh-out-loud hilarious, or shocking moments from the war zone of medicine. Discover the manic antics and incredible skills of ER doctors when a girlfriend's smooch nearly becomes a kiss of death... a farmer's severed foot hitches a ride to the hospital...a premature baby fights valiantly for life... and all the unforgettable cases that come through the swinging doors of the emergency room.

"Funny, sad, shocking, and sometimes almost unbelievable."
—Kirkus Reviews

EMERGENCY!
MARK BROWN, M.D.

Coming in August 1997
from St. Martin's Paperbacks!